Do-it-**Yourself**
BASICS

Save Money • Solve Problems • Improve Your Home

THE BASICS EVERYONE CAN MASTER

D1401766

Reader's Digest

New York, NY/Montreal

Do-It-Yourself Basics

Content Management Mary Flanagan
Design Elizabeth Tunnicliffe
Page Layout David Farr
Proofreading Judy Arginteanu

Text, photography and illustrations for *Do-It-Yourself Basics* are based on articles previously published in *Family Handyman* magazine (2915 Commers Dr., Suite 700, Eagan, MN 55121, familyhandyman.com). For information on advertising in *Family Handyman* magazine, call (646) 518-4215.

Do-It-Yourself Basics is published by Trusted Media Brands, Inc. ©2021

Family Handyman ISBN: 978-1-62145-540-0 (dated)
Family Handyman ISBN: 978-1-62145-541-7 (undated)

Front cover credit: Alistair Berg/Getty Images
Back cover credit: Whitestorm/Getty Images

Address any comments to:
feedback@familyhandyman.com

A Note to Our Readers
All do-it-yourself activities involve a degree of risk. Skills, materials, tools and site conditions vary widely. Although the editors have made every effort to ensure accuracy, the reader remains responsible for the selection and use of tools, materials and methods. Always obey local codes and laws, follow manufacturer instructions and observe safety precautions.

Pricing
Professional services and supplies can vary widely depending on the market. Those listed are average costs and are just a guide to cost savings.

Family Handyman

EDITORIAL
Chief Content Officer Nick Grzechowiak
Editor-in-Chief Gary Wentz
Managing Editor Donna Bierbach
Assigning Editor Berit Thorkelson
Associate Assigning Editor Mary Flanagan
Associate Editors Bill Bergmann, Mike Berner, Jay Cork, Brad Holden, Jason Ingolfsland
Contributing Copy Editor Peggy Parker
Contributing Editors Spike Carlsen, Rick Muscoplat
Lead Carpenter Josh Risberg
Editorial Services Associate Peggy McDermott

ART
Creative Director Vern Johnson
Art Directors Mariah Cates, Jenny Mahoney
Graphic Designer Andrea Sorensen
Photographer Tom Fenenga

Trusted Media Brands, Inc.
President & Chief Executive Officer
Bonnie Kintzer

PRINTED IN CHINA

1 2 3 4 5 6 7 8 9 10

Safety first – always!

Tackling home improvement projects and repairs can be endlessly rewarding.
But as most of us know, with the rewards come risks.
The good news is, armed with the right knowledge, tools and procedures, homeowners
can minimize risk. As you go about your projects and repairs, stay alert for these hazards:

Aluminum wiring

Aluminum wiring, installed in about 7 million homes between 1965 and 1973, requires special techniques and materials to make safe connections. This wiring is dull gray, not the dull orange characteristic of copper. Hire a licensed electrician certified to work with it. For more information go to cpsc.gov and search for "aluminum wiring."

Spontaneous combustion

Rags saturated with oil finishes like Danish oil and linseed oil, and oil-based paints and stains can spontaneously combust if left bunched up. Always dry them outdoors, spread out loosely. When the oil has thoroughly dried, you can safely throw them in the trash.

Vision and hearing protection

Safety glasses or goggles should be worn whenever you're working on DIY projects that involve chemicals, dust and anything that could shatter or chip off and hit your eye. Sounds louder than 80 decibels (dB) are considered potentially dangerous. Sound levels from a lawn mower can be 90 dB, and shop tools and chain saws can be 90 to 100 dB.

Lead paint

If your home was built before 1979, it may contain lead paint, which is a serious health hazard, especially for children 6 and under. Take precautions when you scrape or remove it. Contact your public health department for detailed safety information or call (800) 424-LEAD (5323) to receive an information pamphlet. Or visit epa.gov/lead.

Smoke and carbon monoxide (CO) alarms

The risk of dying in reported home structure fires is cut in half in homes with working smoke alarms. Test your smoke alarms every month, replace batteries as necessary and replace units that are more than 10 years old. As you make your home more energy-efficient and airtight, existing ducts and chimneys can't always successfully vent combustion gases, including potentially deadly carbon monoxide (CO). Install a UL-listed CO detector, and test your CO and smoke alarms at the same time.

Five-gallon buckets and window covering cords

From 1996 to 1999, 58 children under age 5 drowned in 5-gallon buckets. Always store them upside down and store ones containing liquid with the covers securely snapped.

According to Parents for Window Blind Safety, 599 children have been seriously injured or killed in the United States since 1986 after becoming entangled in looped window treatment cords. For more information, visit pfwbs.org or cpsc.gov.

Working up high

If you have to get up on your roof to do a repair or installation, always install roof brackets and wear a roof harness. If you have to work on a ladder on the second story or higher, remember the three points of contact rule: Always have two hands and one foot or two feet and one hand on the ladder.

Asbestos

Texture sprayed on ceilings before 1978, adhesives and tiles for vinyl and asphalt floors before 1980, and vermiculite insulation (with gray granules) all may contain asbestos. Other building materials, made between 1940 and 1980, could also contain asbestos. If you suspect that materials you're removing or working around contain asbestos, contact your health department or visit epa.gov/asbestos for information.

Buried utilities

A few days before you dig in your yard, have your underground water, gas and electrical lines marked. Just call 811 or go to call811.com.

➤ **For additional information about home safety, visit mysafehome.org.
This site offers helpful information about dozens of home safety issues.**

Contents

Fix It

Fix a leaky toilet

YOUR COST: $20

**SAVINGS:
$100**

COMPLEXITY
Moderate

TOOLS
Locking pliers
Drill/driver (cordless)
Hacksaw
Hammer drill

MATERIALS
Flange components
Wax ring
Water closet bolts
Silicone caulk
Plastic toilet shims

If your toilet is leaking around the base, there's a problem with the toilet-to-flange connection. It may be as simple as a wax ring that needs replacement. It's important to stop leaks as soon as possible; even minor ones can cause substantial damage over time. Here are the most common problems you'll find under the toilet and how to address them.

Flange fix-it options

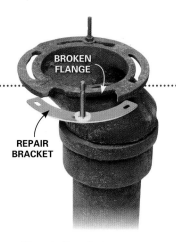

BROKEN FLANGE

REPAIR BRACKET

Two-part repair ring

Steel flanges that surround plastic flanges can rust away. The easiest solution is to install a two-part (or hinged) ring that locks under the plastic rim. Badly corroded steel rings can be pried and peeled away. If you have to get aggressive, cut it away with an angle grinder or oscillating tool fitted with a metal-cutting blade.

Repair Brackets

Cast iron flanges often break on one or both sides. If only the bolt slot is damaged, slip a repair bracket under the cast iron lip. It will be held in place by the unbroken cast iron lip and provide a new slot for the flange bolt.

Eared reinforcement ring

If you have just a small amount of rot surrounding the flange, or screws won't be able to grip the wood under a repair flange, you might get away with an eared reinforcement ring. The ears may extend beyond the rot enough to get a good grip in the subfloor for the screws. Use six 1-1/2-in. No. 8 oval-head stainless steel screws to anchor it in wood. If you have concrete, use 1-1/4-in. flat-head concrete screws.

EAR

BROKEN FLANGE

REPAIR FLANGE

Repair ring

Plastic flanges often bend or break, but there's an easy fix. Just screw a stainless steel repair ring over the plastic flange with at least four 1-1/2-in. stainless steel screws. Consider doing this even if you find that the flange is in good shape and you only need to replace the wax ring. It's cheap insurance against trouble. The repair ring raises the flange about 1/4 in., so before you install the ring, rest it over the flange and then see if the toilet rocks when you set it on top. If it does, you'll need to shim under the toilet to allow for the extra height.

STAINLESS STEEL RING

BROKEN FLANGE

Repair flange

If the flange is in bad shape, you can install a plastic flange that slips inside (shown above). Home centers carry one or two versions of these. Or you can add a brass ring similar to the stainless steel ring shown at left. If necessary, break away the cast iron flange with a cold chisel.

Buy every flange fix sold!

You never know what you're going to find when you pull the toilet, so you have to be prepared so you can get your toilet working again fast. You can always return the items you don't use. (Don't buy the cast iron repair parts unless you have cast iron drain lines.) In addition to the flange fixes, get two wax rings, a new set of brass toilet flange bolts, plastic toilet shims and a tube of tub/tile caulk.

STAINLESS STEEL RIM

Choose flanges with stainless steel rims

If you have access under the toilet, replacing a bad or corroded flange is sometimes the best and easiest solution. Because all plastic flanges are prone to breakage, and plastic flanges with ordinary steel rims are prone to rotting away, the best choice is a plastic flange surrounded with stainless steel. Go downstairs and investigate. Depending on access, you may need elbows, more pipe and a coupling to tie in the new one.

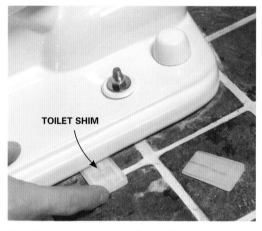

TOILET SHIM

Don't ignore a rocking toilet!

If your toilet is rocking or wobbling, don't ignore it, even if it's not leaking. Eventually the wax ring/ toilet base seal will fail and you'll have a leak. Shim under the toilet with plastic toilet shims until it's steady. Trim the shims and snug up the flange nuts. Then caulk around the base of the toilet with tub/tile caulk.

How a wax ring works

A wax ring is the most commonly used seal between the toilet and the toilet flange. There are synthetic versions, but traditional wax rings (made from real beeswax) are the go-to choice for most plumbers—pros and amateurs alike.

When the toilet is set, the wax is compressed and reshaped to form a watertight seal. Because the wax doesn't harden or degrade, the seal will last for a very long time if the toilet is set properly and firmly bolted down.

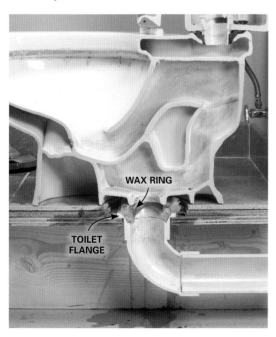

WAX RING

TOILET FLANGE

Dealing with floor rot

If your toilet has been leaking for some time, you're likely to have rot. Finished flooring traps water, which accelerates and spreads the problem. The rot can range from a little bit around the flange to a full-blown case that requires tearing up the flooring and replacing subflooring and possibly framing.

FLANGE SUPPORT BRACKET

Moderate rot

If the rot extends beyond the range of an eared flange but is still contained within the footprint of the toilet, step up to a flange support bracket. These transfer the load past the rotted areas of the subfloor.

NEW WOOD

Extensive rot

Don't freak out if you have bad floor rot. It's easier than you think to cut out the bad flooring and replace it with new wood and additional framing if needed. Just make sure you go far enough to cover the entire area of rotted wood. Bad framing can usually be left in place and reinforced with new 2-by material, if you can screw it into solid wood. Don't worry about removing the rotted framing. With the leak fixed, the rot won't continue. The worst part is that you'll also need to replace the finished floor.

Stop leaks under the sink

Before you can stop a leak, you have to find its source. That can be tricky. Water that escapes your pipes can travel a long way before it drops onto your cabinet's floor.

Here's how a drip detective tracks the source of a leak: Fill both bowls of the sink with lukewarm water, not cold. (Cold water can cause beads of condensation to form on the pipes, making it impossible to find the leak.) Then get under the sink with a trouble light. Dry off all the pipes and examine the seals around the basket strainers. If you don't see any droplets forming, remove both sink stoppers and watch for telltale dribbles. Joints are the most likely source of leaks, but old metal pipes can develop pinhole leaks anywhere, especially in the trap.

If you can't find any leaks in the drain system, check the water supply lines that serve the faucet. Finally, check for "splash leaks," spots where water seeps under the sink rim or faucet base. To find these leaks, use a rag to dribble water around the faucet and sink rim, then get underneath and look for drips.

1. Straighten pipes and tighten nuts

The washers that seal pipe joints won't hold water unless one section runs straight into the other. The "ground" joint on the trap has no washer, but it too will leak if it's misaligned (see p. 17). Eyeball the leaking joint to check its alignment. If it's crooked, simply loosen the nut, straighten the pipe and retighten. Since the whole assembly is interconnected, you might misalign one joint while straightening another. Don't be surprised if you end up loosening and tightening several joints to straighten just one.

If a joint is aligned but leaks anyway, tighten the slip nut. Use two slip-joint pliers on metal pipes: one to hold the pipe, the other to tighten the nut. If you have old metal pipe, you might find that it has worn thin and collapses when you put a pair of pliers on it. With plastic pipe, hand-tighten first. If that doesn't stop the leak, use pliers. But be gentle; plastic threads are easy to strip.

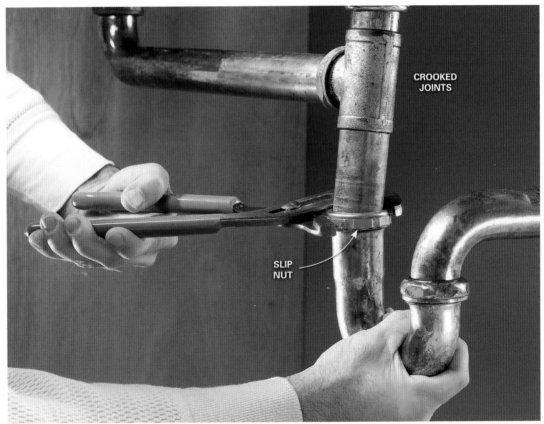

CROOKED JOINTS

SLIP NUT

Loosen slip nuts, then straighten crooked pipes. Retighten metal nuts with slip-joint pliers. With plastic nuts, hand-tighten first. If that doesn't stop the leak, gently snug up the nuts with pliers.

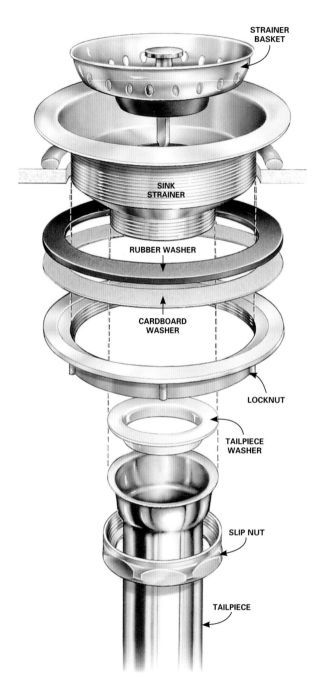

STRAINER BASKET

SINK STRAINER

RUBBER WASHER

CARDBOARD WASHER

LOCKNUT

TAILPIECE WASHER

SLIP NUT

TAILPIECE

Basket strainer assembly

2. Reseal a leaky strainer

The primary seal around a basket strainer is plumber's putty, which doesn't last forever. Over the years it can harden, shrink or crack. Sometimes you can stop a leak by tightening the locknut. But in many cases, the only cure is a new dose of putty. Photos 1–4 below show you how. You can reuse the old strainer if all the parts are in good shape, but it usually makes sense to replace it. Expect to spend at least $20—cheaper strainers are less reliable. Since you have to take apart most of the drain assembly to get at a leaking strainer (**Photo 1**), consider replacing the drain lines if they're old (see p. 16).

The hardest part of this job is unscrewing the old locknut, which is often welded in place by mineral deposits or corrosion. You can use a special wrench designed just for locknuts, called a "spud wrench" or "locknut wrench" (**Photo 2**). Big slip-joint pliers with a 3-1/2-in. jaw opening will work too, plus you can use them for other jobs. Whatever tool you use, you might find that the locknut won't budge. In that case, a single cut with a hacksaw blade is the only solution (**Photo 3**). It's almost impossible to do this without cutting into the strainer threads, so plan on buying a new strainer.

With the locknut removed, pull out the strainer and scrape old putty off the sink with a plastic putty knife. Installing a new strainer is simple (**Photo 4**). Just remember that the rubber washer goes on before the cardboard washer. Tighten the strainer using the same method you used to remove it.

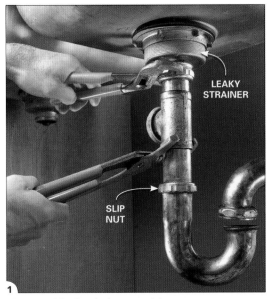

1 Disassemble the drain assembly so you can remove the leaky strainer. Turn slip nuts counterclockwise, using a second set of pliers if necessary to keep the pipes from turning.

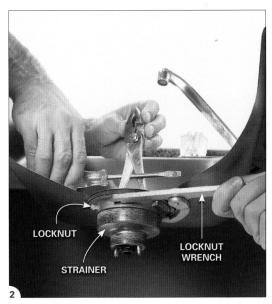

2 Turn the locknut counterclockwise to remove the strainer. Have a helper stick the handles of the pliers into the strainer holes and keep the strainer from turning using a screwdriver.

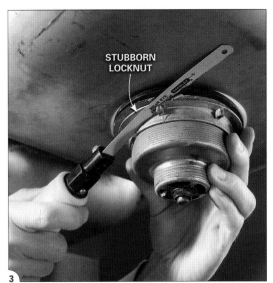

3 Cut the locknut with a hacksaw if you can't unscrew it. Cut at a sharp diagonal angle and be careful not to cut into the sink.

4 Encircle the drain opening with plumber's putty or waterproof caulk. Install the rubber washer and the cardboard washer and tighten the locknut using the same method you used to remove the old one.

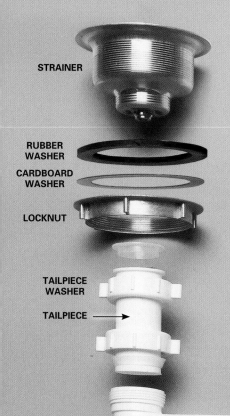

STRAINER

RUBBER WASHER

CARDBOARD WASHER

LOCKNUT

TAILPIECE WASHER

TAILPIECE

WASTE ARM

3. If the pipes are old, replace the whole works

Some leaks can't be stopped with straightening or tightening. Stripped nuts won't tighten, and old washers won't seal because they're stiff and distorted. You could get new nuts, washers or drain parts. Since plastic pipe is so inexpensive and easy to install, the smart, reliable fix is a whole new drain assembly. You can buy everything you need at home centers. Kits for side outlet assemblies (like the one shown here) or center outlet assemblies (where the trap is beneath the center of the sink) contain most of the essential parts. But you might also need:

➤ **Long tailpieces** (Photo 1). The tailpieces that come with kits are often only a couple of inches long.

➤ A **trap arm extender** (Photo 2). The arm that comes with the kit may not reach the drainpipe that protrudes from the wall.

➤ A **dishwasher wye** that has a connection for your dishwasher hose.

➤ A **disposer kit** that allows the waste arm to connect to a garbage disposer.

TAILPIECE WASHER

SLIP NUT

TAILPIECE

1

Attach the tailpiece to the basket strainer, but don't fully tighten it yet; you'll have to remove and cut it later.

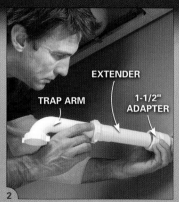

EXTENDER

TRAP ARM

1-1/2" ADAPTER

2

Slide the trap arm into the adapter. Then attach the trap and slide the arm in or out to position the trap directly under the tailpiece. You may need to cut the arm or add an extender.

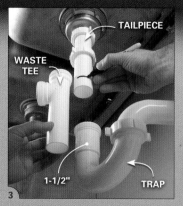

TAILPIECE

WASTE TEE

1-1/2"

TRAP

3

Hold the waste tee alongside the tailpiece about 1-1/2 in. below the top of the trap. Mark the tailpiece 1/2 in. below the top of the tee. Cut both tailpieces to the same length and install them.

Tips for success

➤ You'll have to cut a few pipes: both tailpieces, the waste arm and maybe the trap arm. A fine-tooth hacksaw works best.

➤ When in doubt, mark and cut pipes a bit long. Better to cut twice than cut too short and make an extra trip to the hardware store.

➤ Don't forget to insert tailpiece washers **(Photo 1)**. Other joints require cone washers. The only joint without a washer is the ground joint at the trap.

➤ Connect everything loosely until the whole assembly is complete. Then tighten all the slip nuts.

➤ Hand-tighten the slip nuts. If any joints leak when you test the new assembly, tighten them slightly with slip-joint pliers.

➤ Lastly, check for leaks. To see how, search for "finish a plumbing job" at familyhandyman.com.

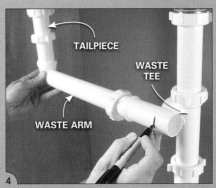

Slip the waste arm onto the second tailpiece, make it extend about 3/4 in. into the tee and mark it. Cut and install it.

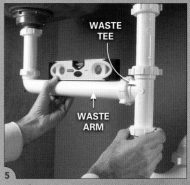

Loosen the slip nuts and slide the tee up or down so the waste arm slopes slightly down toward the tee. Tighten all the nuts.

pro tips!

➤ Brush a little Teflon pipe thread sealant on male threads. It lubricates the threads and makes slip nuts much easier to tighten. Check the label to make sure the sealant is safe for plastic.

Fix a warped cabinet door

While moving into a new house, I noticed one of the tall cabinet doors in the kitchen was badly warped. Rather than replace the door, I decided to fix it with a little heat. This can be tricky, and it's not going to work 100% of the time, but it beats the alternative of having to build a new door.

This technique requires two clamps and a few blocks of wood. I screwed down two blocks for clamping each end of the door, and another as a fulcrum to bend the door against. As clamping pressure is increased on the ends, the door is bent against the warp.

Here's where the heat gun come in. It's important to heat the entire thickness of the wood to an even temperature, not just the surface. To do this without damaging the finish, slowly apply heat to both sides of the door. I used an infrared thermometer to monitor the surface temp, which needed to be 130 degrees F or less. Running the heat gun back and forth along the edge of the door for about 30 minutes, I gently increased clamping pressure, bending a little farther than I thought necessary. Whenever wood is bent with heat, "springback" is to be expected; the wood will relax back to the desired position.

Meet the Expert Jay Cork
has been a carpenter,
cabinetmaker and craftsman
for more than 20 years.

Before

After

FULCRUM

Two solutions for a bouncy floor

If your floor has engineered I-joists and feels a bit "springy" when you walk on it, the fix is relatively easy if you have access to the underside of the joists. You can install either bridging or a layer of plywood. Try bridging first. Just nail short I-joist sections between your existing joists **(Photo 1)**. To prevent squeaks, apply construction adhesive to the top side of the bridging where it contacts your floor. If the joist span is shorter than 14 ft., install one row of bridging at the midpoint. If the span is longer than 14 ft., install two rows of bridging, dividing the span into thirds.

I-JOIST

BRIDGING

1
Toenail a line of I-joist blocks between the joists across the full length of the room.

If the floor is still bouncy, glue and screw 1/2-in. plywood to the bottom of the joists (**Photo 2**). Start the first row at a corner, then stagger subsequent rows so the seams don't fall on the same joists. The drawback to this method is that you have to leave ceiling access to plumbing and gas valves, electrical boxes and other fixtures. Of course, the surest method is to install a beam and posts near the mid-span, but they'll be obstacles in the room below.

CONSTRUCTION
ADHESIVE

1/2" PLYWOOD

2

Fasten 4 x 8-ft. sheets of 1/2-in. plywood to the underside of the I-joists with 1-1/2-in. screws.

Patch a textured ceiling

We're not going to ask how you managed to step through your living room ceiling. But we can tell you that pros fix that mistake quite often, charging hundreds of dollars to patch the hole and retexture it. But you can do the job yourself for less than $100. You'll have to paint the entire ceiling afterward, and even then the patched area won't match perfectly; even a pro can't achieve that. Perfection calls for scraping off and retexturing the entire ceiling after the patch is complete.

You'll only need a small piece of drywall and a couple of scraps of any 3/4-in.-thick wood or plywood, plus standard taping supplies and materials. And you'll need to rent a texture gun. But first, scrape off a small sample of

INSIDE OF FRAMING

TRUSS FINDER

BETWEEN FRAMING

DRYWALL SAW

1

No power saws for this step. Probe with a nail to find the framing on either side of the breakout. Mark the cut between the framing, then make those two cuts until you hit the framing. Then cut alongside the framing at the sides.

TRUSS

NAILING
CLEAT

NEW
VAPOR
BARRIER

2

Patch the hole. Screw 3/4-in.-thick cleats to the sides of the trusses and replace or repair the vapor barrier. Then patch in a fresh piece of drywall.

6" DRYWALL KNIFE

MUD PAN

SPRAYER
WITH
WATER

3

Reapply texture. Wet the texture on the edges of your patch and allow it to soak in for several minutes before you scrape. Tape the joints and then reapply texture.

your texture material and find a match for it at a home center. If you can't find it there, try a local drywall supplier.

Start by cutting out the damaged area. Avoid cutting the vapor barrier, or reseal it with red moisture barrier tape if you do. Screw backer boards above the unsupported drywall ends of the enlarged hole and install the new patch **(Photo 2)**.

Mist water over the surrounding ceiling texture in an area about 24 in. out from the patch to soften it so you can scrape it off to prep for the taping work **(Photo 3)**. Then tape, mud and skim-coat the entire patch. Sand it smooth and you're ready to spray.

Rent a professional spray texture gun and practice on scrap drywall or cardboard. Apply a light coat of texture and add more in stages until you get a match. Lightly blend it into the existing texture.

ADJUSTMENT SCREW

1

Turn the adjustment screws counterclockwise and lower the door frame until it rests on the track.

Align a patio screen door

There you are, balancing a tray full of burgers fresh from the grill, struggling to open the sticking patio screen door. Badly aligned rollers cause the screen door to bind and stick when it's opened or closed. Eventually this stresses the corner joints of the door, and if they open or loosen up, the door is shot. But you can adjust the door to run smoothly in minutes with just a screwdriver. You'll find two adjustment screws at the bottom of the door, one at each end, that lift and lower separate rollers. (Inspect the rollers for damage. Get new ones at home centers or by visiting Blaine Window Hardware at blainewindow.com. First lower the door to the track **(Photo 1)**, then raise it evenly **(Photo 2)**. Still runs rough? Clean the track. Chances are, leaves, grit or other debris is clogging it.

....

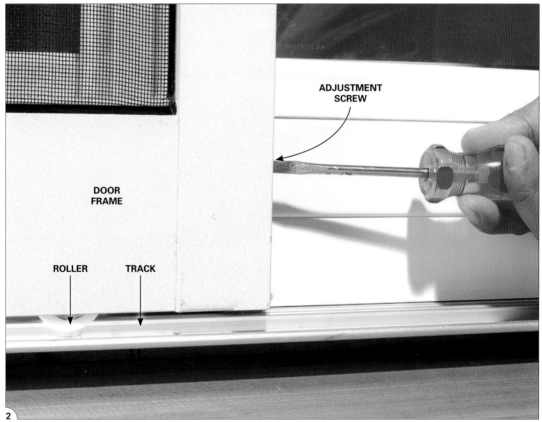

ADJUSTMENT SCREW

DOOR FRAME

ROLLER   TRACK

2

Raise one roller until it lifts the door off the track approximately 1/4 in. Slowly raise the second roller on the other end until the gap between the bottom of the door and the track is even. Make sure there's a gap between the top of the screen frame and the upper track as well.

10 best 10-minute DIY fixes

Save money or prevent future expenses with these
10-minute fixes you can do yourself.

1. Cloudy headlight lenses. You don't have to replace cloudy head-
lights. Buy a headlight restoration kit at any auto parts store and
follow the sanding and buffing instructions.

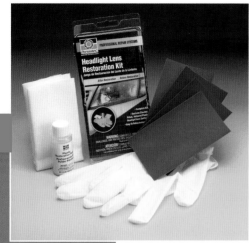

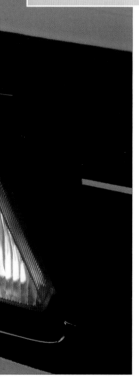

2. Sticking or slow power windows. Give each window channel a shot of dry Teflon or silicone spray lubricant. Then run the window up and down a few times to spread the lubricant.

3. Avoid iced-up wipers. Install winter wiper blades. They're covered by a rubber boot that prevents ice from building up in the wiper and provides streak-free wiping.

4. Defroster grid out of action. Yes, you can fix this yourself. Pick up a Permatex Quick Grid repair kit at any auto parts store. Follow the instructions and you'll be defrosting in no time.

5. Clogged radiator fins. Disconnect the electrical connectors to your electric cooling fans and remove the fasteners. Lift out the entire fan assembly. Then use a garden hose and nozzle to spray the back of the radiator. That will dislodge the gunk stuck to the front side and provide better cooling. Reinstall the fan assembly.

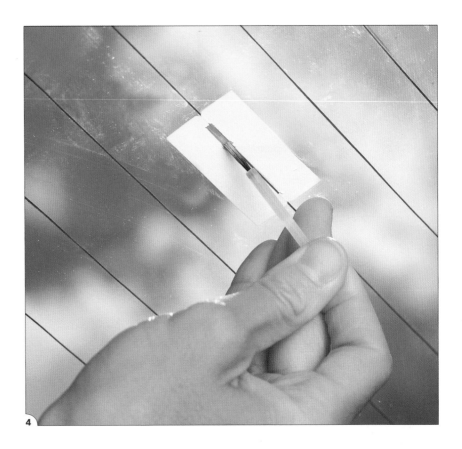

4

6. Squeaky door hinges. Rusty hinges wear faster, causing the door to sag and not close properly. Replacing the hinges can be costly. A quick spray of white lithium grease is all you need to keep them from wearing out.

7. Prevent false ABS trouble codes. Anti-lock brake sensors contain a magnet that can pick up metallic road debris and set off a false "trouble code." Use a rag to wipe the debris off the sensor any time you have your wheels off.

8. Rattling exhaust pipe. Replace exhaust clamps and brackets at the first sign of rust-through or rattling. They're cheap and easy to install, and they protect other exhaust components from vibration damage.

9. Fix paint chips and scratches right away. Use these cool applicator tools and a can of touch-up paint to prevent rust.

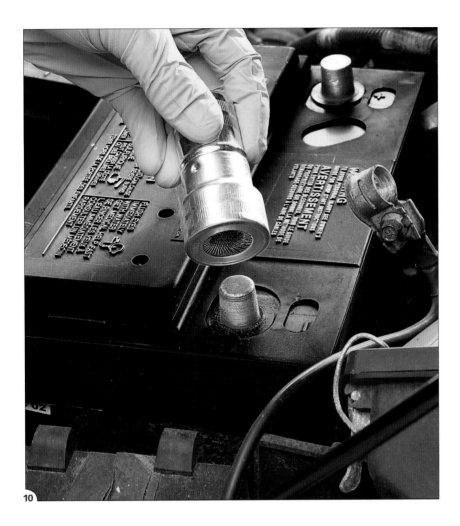

10.

10. Corroded battery terminals. Corrosion puts added strain on your charging system and can mess with computer-controlled systems. Cleaning is your cheapest insurance against electrical problems.

pro tips!

➤ **Don't mix different types of coolant.** Green, yellow, red, orange and blue coolants create cool "mud" when mixed. Cost of a new heater core: $400 to $1,000.

➤ **Don't put E-85 in a "non-flex-fuel" car.** This little mistake will cost you the price of a tow, a fuel tank and fuel line flush, a new fuel filter and a new tank of gas. Expect to pay about $400 for this "oops."

Chapter 2
Clean It

Removing
concrete
stains

Paint stains

Cleaning old paint from concrete is similar to stripping paint from wood. Buy the same types of paint strippers. If you're working outdoors or in a detached garage (with the door open) and want fast results, you can use a methylene chloride–type stripper. The active ingredient will be listed on the can. **Caution:** Methylene chloride can be hazardous. Use only in a well-ventilated area. And wear a respirator equipped with a fresh organic vapor cartridge **(Photo 1)**.

If you use a safer, slow-acting stripper, expect to wait several hours for it to work.

Mix absorbent material into the stripper **(Photo 1)**. Thick strippers won't need much. You can add more paint stripper to the paste after you apply it to keep it actively working on stubborn paint. Scraping with a hard plastic scraper may also help. But let the stripper do most of the work. After scraping, let paint residue dry and toss it into the trash.

1

Add paint stripper to an absorbent material to make a creamy paste. Spread a 1/4- to 1/2-in. layer of paste over the paint stain. Then wait 10 to 20 minutes while the stripper loosens the paint stain.

2

Scrape off the paste and loosened paint with a plastic scraper. Spread a second application if necessary.

3

Scrub area with a nylon brush, scouring powder and water to remove softened paint particles still stuck in the rough concrete.

4

Rinse with plenty of water. Continue scrubbing with a nylon brush to finish cleaning.

Oil and grease stains

You can't scrub oil and grease stains away. The trick is to draw them up out of the concrete. To do this, mix trisodium phosphate (or a TSP substitute) with water and an absorbent material to make a smooth paste. The cleaner slowly soaks into the concrete and breaks up the old oil, and the absorbent material captures it. Once the paste dries, the cleaning action stops, and you can scrape and sweep it away **(Photo 3)**. Either throw it away or renew it with more TSP and water and reapply it for deeper cleaning. Use a nylon brush for cleanup **(Photo 4)**. A wire brush may leave steel particles, which can cause rust stains.

Patience is the key. Old, long-neglected stains may require two or three applications for complete removal. And even then, some stains might still show, or the freshly cleaned area might look slightly different from the surrounding concrete.

Pour 1 oz. trisodium phosphate (or TSP substitute) and a cup of water into a small bucket and mix. Add about a cup of absorbent material and mix to make a creamy paste. Wear eye protection and rubber gloves.

2 Spread a 3/8-in. thick layer of the paste over the stain. Allow the paste to dry for about 24 hours.

3 Scrape and brush off the powdery residue and either reuse it or dump it in your trash.

4 Scrub the area with water and a nylon brush. Rinse with a garden hose.

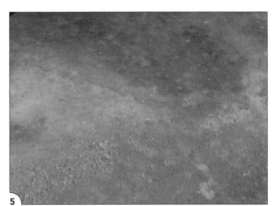

5 Compare the stained area with the surrounding concrete. Repeat the process a second (and perhaps third) time to fully remove the stain.

pro tips!

Buying absorbent materials

You have a variety of options for absorbent materials. For small stains, simply use baby powder or powdered talc. For larger stains, you'll need a bulk material. One good choice is diatomaceous earth, sold as a filtering agent for swimming pools. It's available from most pool supply stores (intheswim.com).

Fuller's Earth is a finely ground clay that also works well for making a paste. It is available at amazon.com, but it's expensive.

Cat litter is also a good absorbent; however, it's too coarse to make a good paste unless you crush it into a powder. The same goes for the absorbent materials that are designed to soak up oil spills.

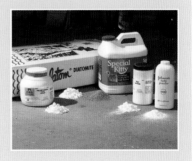

Rust stains

Rust is really tough to get out, because no simple solvent will dissolve it. One effective way to remove rust from concrete is to dissolve the surface layer of concrete using a mild muriatic acid solution. (Muriatic acid is available at many home centers and full-service hardware stores.) Working with an acid solution requires certain safety precautions:

➤ Wear rubber boots, goggles and rubber gloves. Also wear a respirator with a cartridge rated for acid vapor.

➤ Maintain good ventilation. Open doors and windows and add a fan for better air movement **(Photo 1)**.

➤ Keep a 5-gallon bucket of clean water handy to quickly wash away any spill on bare skin.

➤ When mixing, always pour the chemical into the water, never the water into the chemical. And use only glass or plastic containers (no metal).

➤ Cover nearby areas with plastic to protect them from splashes.

Add 1/4 cup of muriatic acid to 2 cups of water in a large, shallow plastic pan. Always pour acid into water, never water into acid. Mask nearby materials with plastic covering to protect them from splashes.

1

- ➤ Read the manufacturer's dilution guidelines on the label and follow them if they're different from ours **(Photo 1)**.
- ➤ Store extra acid out of reach of children and pets.

The acid dissolves the cement in the surface layer of concrete. You want to minimize this etching process, so start with a light application and observe the results. You'll see the solution begin bubbling almost immediately **(Photo 2)**. After the bubbling stops, scrub lightly with a long-handled nylon brush to see if the rust disappears.

Once the entire area is clean, thoroughly rinse it with lots of water to dilute any remaining acid and remove all traces of residue **(Photo 3)**. Direct the rinse water away from your lawn or plants.

After cleaning with acid, play it safe. Thoroughly rinse your protective gear, wash your clothing and take a shower to make sure all traces are washed away.

Since each acid cleaning erodes the concrete surface, it's far better for your garage floor if you avoid the problem in the first place. Hang up wet tools and other items that'll cause rust. And protect the floor with paint or a sealer.

....

2

Spread the acid solution over the rusted area. Allow it to stand five minutes while the acid works. Reapply as needed, scrubbing more in stubborn areas.

3

Rinse and scrub the area thoroughly, using plenty of fresh water to flush away all traces of residue.

4

Acid treatment leaves the surface of the concrete slightly rougher, like fine sandpaper. Once it's dry, seal your floor to reduce future staining.

Extreme cleaning

You probably don't think of cleaning as home improvement, but a thorough cleaning really is a powerful way to improve your home. Things that look old, worn and in need of replacement sometimes just need a good scrubbing! Some of us at Family Handyman have learned that lesson recently.

If you're buying

The house my wife and I bought was pretty dirty, which triggered some buyer's remorse. So we spent a long, hard day cleaning. It was worth it. The grime left by the previous owners is gone, and the place feels like ours.

Mike Berner
Associate Editor

If you're selling

To show our house in the best light possible, we cleaned everything and every corner. Dirt is unattractive, and somebody else's dirt is especially so. You'll get more and better offers if potential buyers see your house as "move-in ready."

Marcia Roepke
Art Director

If you're staying

A long weekend of cleaning cut my list of remodeling chores in half. The grout, the kitchen sink and fixtures, the entryway walls—they didn't need a redo. A deep cleaning made them look like new. Well, almost.

Gary Wentz
Editor-in-chief

pro tips!

Declutter first

Cleaning your house is far easier once you remove clutter, and that's something most of us need to do anyway. If you're selling, don't just put everything in the garage. That's a turnoff for potential buyers. Move your stuff off site.

➤ **Donate it.** Donating your goods is a nice way to get rid of usable items without the hassles of selling them. Perfect if you have a lot of stuff and limited time.

➤ **Sell it.** If you have time and you'd like to make a little extra cash, sell unwanted things online. Keep in mind that you'll have to check messages and be available for people coming over to buy your stuff. It can be a big hassle.

➤ **Put it on the curb.** Setting free stuff on the curb is probably the quickest and easiest way to get rid of it. People will take anything that's free! The drawback is that if you itemize deductions on your tax returns, you won't get a receipt to count it as a charitable donation. You can also list free items on craigslist.com.

➤ **Trash it.** If you have a lot of junk, throwing it all in a dumpster or Bagster bag is an easy and gratifying experience. The rental company can help you determine what size dumpster you need.

➤ **Store it.** For the items you're keeping but not using for staging, mobile storage containers are the way to go. Have one dropped at your house, fill it up, and then the company will haul it off to a temporary storage facility or your new home. The cost varies depending on the container size and the distance of the move.

Focus on the bathroom

Cleaning the bathroom might take you more time than the rest of the house combined. But it's essential, especially if you're selling. If there's one room potential buyers are extra-picky about, it's the bathroom. It should be spotless.

Glass shower doors: Built-up soap scum seems impossible to remove. Pick up polishing compound at a home center or an auto parts store and use it with an auto buffer to polish off the offending scum. If you don't own a buffer, you can buy one or borrow one from a gearhead friend. If possible, take the doors out to the garage to avoid messing up the bathroom.

Caulking: Trying to clean caulk often isn't worth the effort. If it's covered with mold or mildew, just cut it out and recaulk.

Exhaust fan: Turn on the fan and blast out the dust with "canned air." The fan will blow the dust outside. This works on the return air grilles of your central heating/cooling system too. Run the system so the return airflow will carry the dust to the filter. You'll find canned air at home centers, usually in the electrical supplies aisle.

Rust stains: To clean rust from toilets and other porcelain surfaces, add three parts water to one part rust remover (Acid Magic is one brand we like). Use a sprayer, brush or foam pad to apply the mixture to the rust stains, then watch them dissolve. Rinse with clear water. You can also use it full strength for stubborn stains. Avoid getting the acid on metal parts because they can discolor. Acid Magic is available online and at hardware stores.

Faucets and fixtures:
Scrub faucets and fixtures with a calcium, lime and rust remover, such as CLR, and an old toothbrush.

Tile grout: Try a bleach pen to transform your grout from grungy to great. This method is tedious, but the payoff is crisp, clean grout lines. Use the pen to "draw" bleach across the grout lines. The pen allows you to target the grout without getting bleach all over the tile. Wait 10 minutes and then rinse.

Tile: Magic Eraser sponges (or other brands) make short work of cleaning tile. Just dampen the sponge and rub it on the offending mess. In most cases, the mess will come right off. These sponges are especially useful for removing ground-in dirt from porous floor tile and cleaning those pesky nonslip strips in the bottom of your tub.

pro tips!

Dig into the details

Some cleaning jobs get overlooked, either because we're so used to these areas not being clean, or because we just don't like doing them. Pay attention to the following:

- Ceiling fan blades
- Light fixtures
- Baseboards/trim/door frames
- Handrails
- Furniture feet
- Fingerprints
- Furnace exterior
- Water heater exterior
- Exposed pipes and ductwork
- Washer and dryer
- Inside cabinets and drawers
- Walls and ceilings
- Curtains
- Under appliances
- Trash cans
- Doorknobs
- Dishwasher
- Throw pillows

Windows

Your windows present the view as well as let in natural light. You can hire a window cleaning service, but if you'd like to do it yourself, go to familyhandyman.com and search for "how to clean windows."

Carpet

If the carpet is reasonably clean, don't go beyond vacuuming it. Carpet is the last thing buyers look at and doesn't give a big return on investment. If there's hardwood underneath, consider removing the carpet.

Get a cleaning service

You can hire a pro to do a deep cleaning. Rather than spending an entire weekend cleaning, you can pay someone to do it for you and consider it part of the cost of staging your house.

Don't clean; replace

Some things just aren't worth the effort to clean. You'll save time and money and get better results by simply replacing the following items with new:

- Shower curtains
- Switch plates
- Mini blinds
- Showerheads

Simply clean

Schar Ward cleans the old-fashioned way—with homemade cleaning solutions, rags made from sheets, and a little elbow grease. With decades of experience, she's tackled dirt, grime and stains that aren't for the faint of heart, and she doesn't think you need fancy new products to clean. With a little knowledge, you can get the job done with many of the household cleaners you probably have lying around. Here are some of her favorite techniques to make your house shine.

....

Meet the Expert Schar Ward has been professionally cleaning homes since 1973. She's the author of Teaching Children to Clean and loves to pass on her knowledge to the next generation.

Prevent mineral buildup with a squeegee. Hard water buildup means hard work later. Schar gives a squeegee to all her customers and tells them to use it after every shower. It makes cleaning showers much easier.

Tips to clean like a pro

KNEEPADS

Ditch the mop

Schar doesn't use a wet mop. She says mops do more harm, spreading dirt everywhere. Instead, she says to clean floors on your hands and knees. First vacuum, then fill a bucket three-quarters full of warm water and 1 tbsp. castile soap. Wash with a terry cloth rag in a 4-sq.-ft. section, dry and repeat, working your way out of the room. Inexpensive, non-marring foam cap kneepads help keep you comfortable while you wash the floor.

Run the dishwasher with vinegar

Dishwashers need to be cleaned if you have hard water. Place a half cup of vinegar on the top rack and run it normally. Do this every few weeks.

A pumice stone gets rid of mineral buildup

Use a pumice stone to remove mineral deposits from toilets, sinks, tubs and oven interiors. Pumice is abrasive enough to grind off the minerals but won't scratch porcelain. Just be sure to keep the end wet. You can use it on grill and oven grates, too. Pumice stones are available at home centers and online.

Tips to clean like a pro

Use heavy books to help remove carpet stains

Spray the stained area with Folex or other carpet stain cleaner, blot it with towels, being sure not to rub, and cover the towels with wax paper. Then place heavy books or other weights on top of the towels. Leave the weights in place overnight and the stain will be gone.

WAX
PAPER

pro tips!

➤ **Make your own rags.** To save money, Schar makes her own rags from sheets she buys at the thrift store. Cut them to size and if you like, hem them so they don't fray. You'll have plenty of rags without paying a premium.

➤ **Wash your rags twice.** If you want a clean house, you need clean rags. Dirty rags harbor all kinds of bacteria, so wash your rags twice—once with bleach and the second time without.

➤ **Forget disposable cloths.** Disposable dust cloths might seem like a good idea, but use a flannel cloth with a little Old English instead. It's just as effective and you'll save money.

➤ **Anything you wash, you dry.** Don't wash surfaces with a cleaner and let them dry on their own; it leaves a sticky residue. Dry everything after washing.

➤ **Lift objects; don't slide.** When dusting, it's easy to move objects around without thinking about how you're moving them, but Schar emphasizes you must lift them rather than sliding. Sliding scratches the finish.

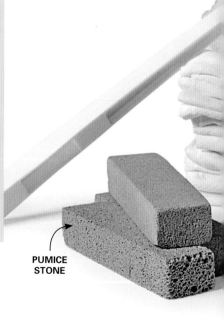

PUMICE
STONE

pro tips!

Don't get overwhelmed

Faced with a whole house to clean, you're more likely to procrastinate, get sidetracked during the job or just give up. So Schar has developed a strategy to make cleaning manageable, approachable and efficient.

➤ **Start with the dirtiest room first.** Tackle the big project first and everything else will seem easy in comparison. Plus, you'll feel better when it's done.

➤ **Work top to bottom, left to right.** When staring a dirty room in the face, you may feel at a loss to know where to start. Schar recommends you work top to bottom, left to right. When you're done, do a quick once over to see if you've missed anything.

➤ **Set a time limit.** Instead of telling the family it's a cleaning day, set a time limit and stick to it. Cleaning isn't so bad when you say you'll do it for two hours rather than all day.

Bowl swab

Schar uses a bowl swab to clean toilets. Standard toilet brushes don't work well for spreading toilet cleaner around the bowl— a little water rinses it right off the bristles. The swab, on the other hand, retains the cleaner and can reach underneath the rim and down the throat of the toilet bowl. Schar also uses a swab to clean tile.

Rags

Schar uses three types of rags: cotton sheets, flannel and terry cloth. The cotton sheets are for drying windows, the flannel is for dusting, and the terry cloth is for scrubbing.

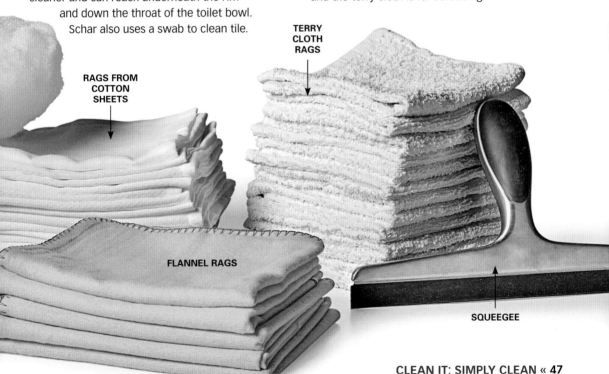

RAGS FROM COTTON SHEETS

TERRY CLOTH RAGS

FLANNEL RAGS

SQUEEGEE

Schar's secret weapons

Shown here are Schar's favorite commercial cleaning products—for removing stubborn mineral deposits, cleaning and protecting wood surfaces, and more. We were surprised to learn that for most cleaning tasks, she prefers to mix her own solutions. Check those out at right.

Old English

To clean and protect wood surfaces, Schar recommends Old English. Its nongreasy formula helps prevent water marks and stains.

Phosphoric acid cleaner

For stubborn mineral deposits on natural stone, porcelain, concrete and masonry, Schar says phosphoric acid cleaner is a must-have. After applying, let it sit for 10 minutes, rinse and you're done. You could use vinegar, but it takes longer.

Murphy Oil Soap

Schar loves using this cleaner on wood floors, but she emphasized that you need to dry the floor afterward.

Folex

Schar has seen plenty of tough carpet stains. She says Folex carpet spot remover has never failed to take out a stain. You can find it online or at home centers.

Use eraser sponges on paint with caution

Eraser sponges like the Magic Eraser have their uses, but be careful on painted surfaces; they can alter the sheen of the paint. Alternatively, use a mix of Murphy Oil Soap and baking soda to clean walls.

Make your own cleaning solutions

Instead of loading up on expensive cleaners, make your own solutions with common household products like vinegar and baking soda. Here are a few of Schar's recipes:

Scrubbing solution

➤ 1-3/4 cups baking soda
➤ 1/2 cup water
➤ 1/2 cup castile soap
➤ A few drops of essential oil

Mix in bowl and stir until it has the consistency of frosting. Store in a pump bottle. Shake well before use. It's effective on pots and pans, sinks, bathtubs and more.

All-purpose spray

Fill a spray bottle with half vinegar and half water. Add 10 drops of scented oil.

Window cleaner

Pour one bottle of club soda in a spray bottle.

Hard-water buildup cleaner

➤ 1 tsp. borax
➤ 1tbsp. castile soap
➤ 2 tbsp. white vinegar
➤ 2 cups water
➤ 5 drops of essential oil

Mix and store in spray bottle.

Carpet freshener

Fill a shaker container three-quarters full of baking soda. Add 10 drops of essential oil. Mix with a fork and sprinkle on carpet. Clean with a vacuum.

Essential oils

Add an essential oil to your cleaning solutions for a fresh scent.

7 Steps to renew your auto interior

Unless you're fastidious about your car's interior, it's usually the last thing on your cleaning list. As the months roll by, grime, wrappers, dust and junk can just pile up. Unfortunately, most of us finally get around to the deep cleaning when we decide to sell the car. But why wait when you can easily get your car looking its best with these tips from professional detailers? Your efforts will be rewarded with a car that looks and feels brand-new.

1. **Vacuum like you mean it.** Slide the seat all the way forward and clean out all the junk underneath. You'll be surprised by what you find. We found a lost cell phone, enough pens and pencils to equip a small office, and enough coins for several vending machine lunches. Vacuum the seats, remove the mats and vacuum the carpet. Use a brush attachment for the dash and door panels. Don't forget to clean out and vacuum those handy door pockets (another source of buried treasure).

1

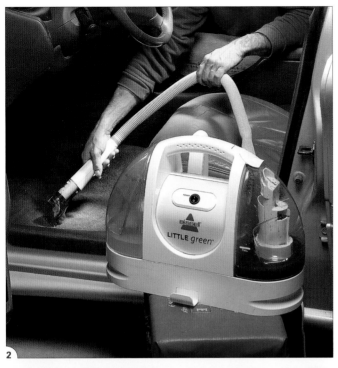

2. **Clean the carpet.** Deep-clean the carpeting and upholstery. Use a carpet cleaning machine to get the dirt that settles deep into the fibers of the carpet. (Clean cloth seats this way as well.) It sprays the carpet with a solution of water and cleaner and then sucks the dirt and grime into a reservoir. A machine like this pays for itself after just a few uses. You can also rent one from a rental center or use a spray-on cleaner and a scrub brush instead.

3. **Clean & condition the seats.** After a few years, you'll notice that the color of the leather or vinyl seats no longer matches that of the rest of the interior. It's not enough just to condition the leather. First spray on leather cleaner and rub vigorously with a clean terry cloth towel. To avoid rubbing the grime back into the seats, keep flipping the cloth to expose a fresh surface. Let the seats dry for an hour and then rub in a leather conditioner like Lexol to keep the leather supple. It's available at discount stores and auto stores.

4. **Remember the recesses.** Detailing means just that—cleaning all the trim lines and recesses. Wrap a cloth around a worn screwdriver (no sharp edges) and spray it with Simple Green or other all-purpose cleaner. Move it gently along the trim lines to pick up dirt, using fresh sections of cloth as you go. Then clean around the buttons and controls, and follow up with a rejuvenator like Armor All.

5. **Brush out the air vents.** These louvers are a real magnet for dust, and a vacuum with a brush attachment just won't get it all. Take an inexpensive paintbrush and give it a light shot of Endust or Pledge furniture polish. Work the brush into the crevices to collect the dust. Wipe the brush off with a rag and move on to the next vent.

4

5

6. **Wash the windows.** Don't forget the top edges. Ever notice that line of grime on the tops of windows when they're partially rolled down? Most people overlook this detail when giving their vehicle a quick wash. A few minutes with Windex and a clean rag is all it takes.

7. **Scrape off old stickers.** While all of your national and state park stickers may call to mind great memories, they can be a visual hazard as they accumulate. The high-quality stickers will pull off if you can get under a corner and carefully pull them free at a 90-degree angle. Others will leave a gummy residue and require a bit more attention. Cover your dash with an old towel and dab on Goo Gone. Then scrape and wipe it off.

Remove and prevent roof algae

PROFESSIONAL COST: $400

YOUR COST: $120

SAVINGS: $280

COMPLEXITY
Simple

TOOLS
Roof safety harness

Boots or shoes with traction

Garden sprayer

Stiff-bristle brush

Garden hose

Crow bar

Hammer

Scissors

MATERIALS
Cleaning solution

Zinc strips

Rubber washer nails

Roof stains make any house stand out—but not in a good way. Luckily, these stains aren't inevitable as a roof ages. They're caused by algae growth in humid, shaded areas, usually with lots of tree cover. While algae won't damage your roof,

it will hurt your home's curb appeal. Fortunately, it's easy and inexpensive to remove and prevent stubborn algae stains yourself. Here's how to clean your roof and make your home stand out in the best way.

Replace your roof with algae-resistant shingles

If you're in the market to reshingle your roof, consider installing algae-resistant shingles. They'll keep your roof looking great and cost about the same as standard shingles.

Meet the Expert Andy Lodge has been in the industry since 1981 and has worked on hundreds of roofing projects around the world. He is now a consultant for IKO Industries.

How to remove roof stains

To see an immediate improvement, you'll need to climb onto your roof, spray it with a cleaning solution and rinse with water. A cleaning solution and water will remove most algae stains right away, but some can be especially difficult. If you have a steep roof, it's best to call a pro. Here's how I cleaned my roof.

1. Mix a homemade solution. To save money, I opted to make my own solution. Commercial roof cleaners are available at most home centers, but they're expensive and won't work any better than a home-made solution. Plus, it's easy to make your own. Mix 15 oz. of an oxygen bleach powder (I used OxiClean Stain Remover, available at home centers for about $12) with 2 gallons of warm tap water in a garden sprayer. Don't use chlorinated bleach; it'll kill the lawn and plants on the ground below.

2. Spray the shingles. Once you're on the roof, start at the edge and spray the shingles with your homemade solution, working your way up to the ridge. A wet roof is a slippery roof, so leave a dry path back to your ladder. Allow the solution to sit for 20 minutes before rinsing. Tough stains may require an additional application and a mild scrubbing with a stiff-bristle brush.

CAUTION

Be safe! Climbing a roof is dangerous. Use a safety harness, wear boots or shoes with good traction and consider installing a slide guard. For more information, search "roof safety" at familyhandyman.com.

3. Rinse with a garden hose. After you've waited for the solution to do its work, douse the roof with a garden hose, clearing suds and algae off the shingles. You'll see a big improvement unless your stains are especially stubborn. Never use a pressure washer to clean the algae; the roof will be clean, but its life will be shortened by the loss of granules.

How to prevent roof stains

A great way to tackle your roof algae problem is to install zinc strip. Zinc is toxic to algae. When rainwater hits the zinc strip, zinc ions run down the shingles, killing algae. It's easy to install and inexpensive, and it does most of the cleaning work for you. You can find a 50-ft. roll of zinc strip at home centers or online for about $35. Here's how to install it.

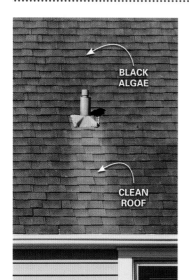

BLACK ALGAE

CLEAN ROOF

You'll often see clean streaks in the shingles below galvanized flashing. That's because the flashing works just like zinc strips: The zinc on the flashing combines with rainwater to kill the algae.

ZINC STRIP LOCATIONS

ZINC STRIP LOCATIONS

Where to install zinc strip. Zinc strips work only on areas directly downhill. So if you have dormers, ungalvanized roof vents, valleys, roofs under gables or any other sections that could obstruct the flow of zinc, install zinc strip in those locations too.

How to install it

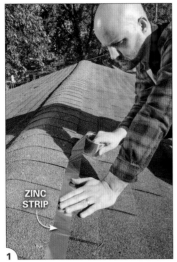

ZINC STRIP

1

Slide it under the shingles. Start at the beginning of the ridge and gently pry up the cap shingles with a crowbar. Roll out 2 ft. of zinc strip and slide it no more than 1 in. under the cap shingles.

2

Fasten under the shingle. Fasten with galvanized rubber washer nails under the shingles. You can also use an exterior construction adhesive. Continue to fasten the zinc strip every 12 in. until you've reached the end of the ridge and then clip it to length with scissors. I found cutting the zinc strip at the end saved time and kept it from flapping around in the wind.

Zinc strip test

Zinc strip is often marketed as a moss, fungus and algae preventer, but not as a remover. However, expert home inspector Reuben Saltzman installed zinc strip on a moss-covered roof to see if it would remove the moss over time. As you can see in the before and after photos, it significantly reduced the moss and algae. So, if you don't mind waiting, you can skip the cleaning and let zinc strip do the job.

SHINGLES BEFORE

18 MONTHS LATER

Chapter **3**

Replace It

Replace a toilet

Whether you're installing a better-flushing toilet or resetting the old one after repairs or remodeling, these tips will help you do it faster and with fewer problems. The job can take less than an hour, but set aside a whole morning in case you run into trouble. Everything you'll need is available at home centers and hardware stores.

Hiring a plumber to replace a toilet typically costs about $150. If there are hidden problems, such as a broken floor flange, that cost can easily double.

PROFESSIONAL COST: $120

YOUR COST: $20
(not including toilet)

SAVINGS: $100

COMPLEXITY
Moderate

TOOLS
Tape measure
Locking pliers
Close-quarters
  hacksaw blade

MATERIALS
Brass bolts and nuts
Toilet flange
Wax ring
Shims

Check the "rough-in." If you're buying a new toilet, you need to know the "rough-in" measurement of the old one. For the vast majority of toilets, the waste pipe is centered about 12 in. from the wall. But with a few models, that measurement is 10 in. or 14 in. To check the rough-in, just measure from the wall to the toilet's hold-down bolts. If that measurement (plus the thickness of the baseboard) isn't approximately 12 in., toilet shopping will be a bit harder. Most home centers carry only one or two 10-in. models and no 14-in. models. If you have to special-order a toilet, be prepared to spend much more.

If there's a door near the toilet, also measure how far the bowl protrudes from the wall. If you replace a standard bowl with an "elongated" model, the door may not close.

Lock down the bolts. Setting a toilet onto the new bolts can be the most frustrating part of the whole installation. The bolts slip and tip as you're straining to align them with the holes in the toilet. And each time you miss, you risk crushing or shifting the wax ring. The plastic slip-on washers sometimes included with bolts help, but they still allow the bolts to move. The best approach is to buy a second set of nuts and washers so you can lock the bolts in place before you set the toilet. To make sure they're in the correct position, set the toilet and check its height and position. Then lift it off and add the wax ring. To make the bolts easier to find, mark their locations with masking tape.

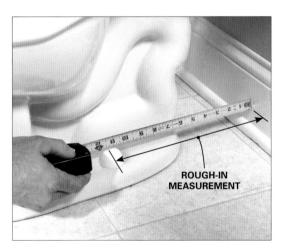

ROUGH-IN
MEASUREMENT

EXTRA NUT
AND WASHER

Cut hold-down bolts.

Don't be surprised if the old nuts that hold the toilet in place won't budge. Years of corrosion can weld them to their bolts. In that case, a hacksaw blade is the solution. You can buy a "close quarters" blade holder at home centers and hardware stores, or just wrap a bare blade with a rag or duct tape. Most toilet bolts and nuts are brass, so they're easy to cut. If the bolt spins, grab it with locking pliers as you cut.

Brass bolts are best. Some metal toilet bolts have a yellowish zinc coating that makes them look like brass. So check the label and make sure you're getting brass bolts and nuts. They won't rust away and they're easier to cut off later. If you need to re-anchor the toilet flange (see p. 65), buy stainless steel screws. They won't corrode like steel or break off like brass while you're driving them.

Flange fixes

A rock-solid toilet flange is the key to a leak-free toilet. The flange is the only thing anchoring the toilet to the floor. If the flange is loose or damaged, the toilet will rock. And a rocking toilet will distort the wax ring and cause leaks. So be sure to scrape off the old wax ring and inspect the flange. Here are some solutions for broken, corroded or loose flanges.

Ear-type ring Loose flanges are usually the result of wood rot. The flange screws simply won't hold in the soft, decayed subfloor. The best solution depends on the extent of the rot. If the rot is only under the flange, use an ear-type repair ring. The ears let you drive screws into firm wood farther away from the flange. Before you install this kind of ring, hold it up to the drain horn on the underside of the toilet. You may have to cut off a couple of ears to make it work with your toilet. If the rot extends well beyond the flange, you'll have to replace a section of the subfloor.

Repair ring Plastic flanges often bend or break, but that's an easy fix. Just screw a stainless steel repair ring over the plastic flange with at least four 1-1/2-in. stainless steel screws. Consider doing this even if the plastic flange is in good shape—it's cheap insurance against future trouble. The repair ring raises the flange by about 1/4 in. So before you install the ring, set it on the flange and set your toilet over it to make sure it fits.

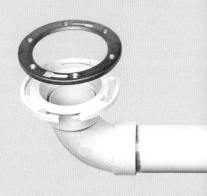

Two-part repair ring Steel flanges attached to plastic hubs can rust away. The easiest solution is a two-part ring that locks onto the plastic just like the old one. To cut away the old flange, use a hacksaw blade or an angle grinder with a metal-cutting wheel. The repair flange is available at some Lowe's stores. To buy online, search for "bay flange."

Repair flange Cast iron flanges can break or corrode. If only the bolt slot is damaged, slip a repair bracket under the flange. If the flange is in bad shape, you can add a brass repair ring similar to the stainless steel ring shown here or install a plastic flange that slips inside. If necessary, break away the cast iron flange with a cold chisel. Home centers carry one or two slip-in flanges. For a wider variety, search online for "replacement toilet flange."

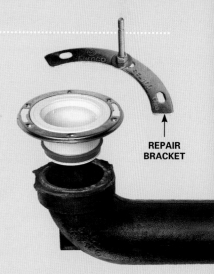

REPAIR BRACKET

Shake your booty to squish the wax. When you set the toilet in place, you have to squish the wax ring until the toilet settles to the floor. DON'T force the toilet down by tightening the nuts on the toilet bolts — that might crack the porcelain base. Instead, sit on the toilet backward with your weight centered over the wax ring. Then wiggle your bottom like a belly dancer until the toilet reaches the floor. But don't go wild. You want to drive the toilet straight down with minimal twisting or shifting of it from side to side. When the toilet reaches the floor, snug down the toilet bolt nuts.

Warning: To avoid ridicule, make sure no one is watching while you perform this maneuver.

Eliminate rocking with shims. A toilet that rocks on an uneven floor will eventually break the wax ring seal and leak. So check for wobbles after you've set the toilet in place and loosely tightened the nuts. For slight wobbles, slip coins or stainless steel washers into the gaps under the toilet. Don't use regular steel washers, which might rust and stain the floor. For larger gaps, use shims. There are plastic shims made especially for toilets, but plastic construction shims like the ones shown here work just as well. When you've eliminated the wobble, tighten the nuts, cut off the shims and caulk around the toilet base. A toilet set on thick vinyl flooring can loosen as the vinyl compresses. In that case, just retighten the nuts a few days after installation.

Don't overtighten the water connections. Do yourself a favor and buy a flexible water supply line. They're a lot easier to install than stiff metal or plastic tubing. Be sure to get one that's covered with stainless steel mesh. For a good seal, hold the hose so it aims straight into the shutoff or fill valve while you're screwing on the connectors. Make them hand-tight, then add another quarter turn with pliers. Connections that are too tight can actually cause leaks or spin the fill valve.

pro tips!

Cut the bolts last

To make positioning a toilet easier, new toilet bolts are extra long. That means you have to cut off the protruding ends later with a hacksaw. But first connect the water line, flush the toilet a couple of times and check for leaks. Leaving the bolts uncut until you've done these final checks lets you easily remove and reset the toilet if you find any problems.

After cutting, double-check the bolts for tightness. Cutting often loosens the nuts a bit.

Replace a dishwasher

PROFESSIONAL COST: $75

YOUR COST: $20
(not including dishwasher)

SAVINGS: $55

COMPLEXITY
Moderate

TOOLS
4-in-1 screwdriver

Adjustable wrench

Level

Pliers

Voltage tester

Floor protection

Screwdriver

Tape measure

Bucket to catch water

MATERIALS
Braided stainless
 steel water line
 (optional)

Teflon tape

Cardboard

Swapping out that old, noisy dishwasher for a new, quiet one is a lot easier than you might think. With a few basic tools and an hour or two, you'll have that new one in and can pocket the $100 to $200 installation fee. There's only one better deal: If installation is part of the purchase price, let the dealer do it!

Here we'll show you how to pull out your old dishwasher, slide in the new one, and make the new water, drain and electrical connections.

In most cases, you won't need any special tools or skills to do a first-class job. Most dishwashers are 24 in. wide, so you won't have to alter cabinets to get the

new one to fit. (If you change sizes, you'll have to alter your cabinets. This requires more advanced carpentry skills that we won't show here.)

You may find that extra layers of flooring have raised the floor height in front of the old dishwasher. This can make it difficult to get the old dishwasher out and the new one in. In some cases, you have to either loosen the countertop or remove flooring. Consider consulting a professional installer if you don't feel confident about the best strategy.

··

Before you start

Get a blanket, an old rug or cardboard to protect your floor while you work. Gather two adjustable wrenches, a screwdriver, a tape measure, a pair of pliers and a level. You'll also need a shallow pan, bucket, sponge and rag to collect water that'll drain from the lines when you disconnect them.

ELECTRICAL BOX

VOLTAGE DETECTOR

BOX COVER

LOWER FRONT PANEL

1

Turn off the power, remove the front panel and use a voltage tester to make sure the power is off. Disconnect the wires and pull the cable from the box.

Turn off the power to the dishwasher at the main panel or unplug it under the sink. Also turn off the water to the dishwasher at the nearest shutoff valve, usually the hot water shutoff under the sink. Or shut it off at the water heater.

Consider removing the cabinet doors from your sink base to make disconnecting the drain lines easier.

Disconnect the electrical cable and water line

The water and electrical connections are underneath the dishwasher, behind a lower front panel that you have to unscrew (**Photo 1**). Always test with a voltage detector to make sure the power is off. When you remove the electrical line from the box, leave the cable clamp on and reuse it on the new dishwasher (**Photo 12**). Sometimes dishwashers are plug-and-cord connected rather than "hard wired" as shown in our photos. If so, disconnect the cord and reuse it on the new dishwasher. If it's in bad condition, buy a new one from an appliance dealer.

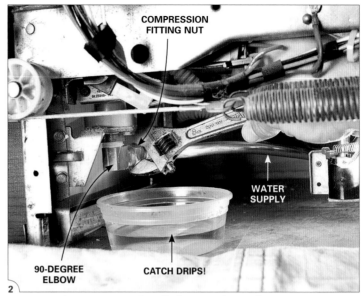

2

Remove the compression fitting nut from the water supply line (water turned off). Note which way the 90-degree elbow points, then unscrew it.

3

Slide the dishwasher drain tube off the inlet arm on the sink drain. Drain it into a bucket. Remove the screws securing the dishwasher to the countertop.

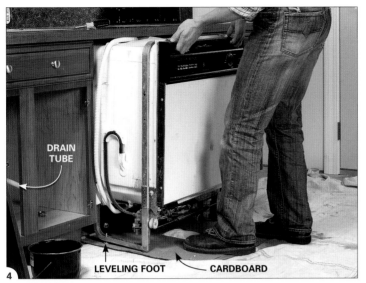

DRAIN TUBE

LEVELING FOOT   **CARDBOARD**

4

Lower the dishwasher and slip cardboard under the feet. Then gently lift and slide the dishwasher out. Work the drain tube out through the side of the cabinet.

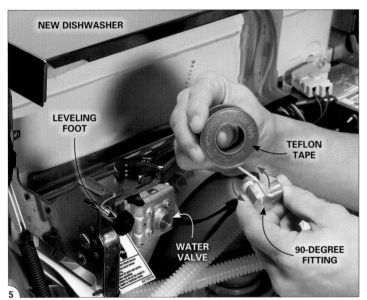

NEW DISHWASHER

LEVELING FOOT

TEFLON TAPE

WATER VALVE

90-DEGREE FITTING

5

Wrap the 90-degree fitting twice with Teflon tape and screw it into the new water valve. Tighten it, aiming the elbow as on the old machine.

Usually, the water supply line is flexible copper or braided stainless steel. In either case, remove the nut securing it to the 90-degree fitting on the dishwasher (**Photo 2**). As long as the nut and ring are in good condition (no nicks or gouges; **Photo 11**), leave them on the line for later reuse. You can bend the copper line slightly, but take care not to kink the line. If you do, you'll have to replace it. Flexible stainless steel lines are a good replacement. Make sure you buy them long enough and with fittings that match the old.

Remove the 90-degree fitting for use on the new dishwasher. It's important to orient it exactly the same direction on the new machine so that the water line feeds directly into it. Otherwise you might kink the line.

Sponge out any standing water inside the dishwasher before removing the drain line under the sink. It's the flexible hose that's clamped to an inlet arm on the sink drain or a garbage disposer (**Photo 3**). As you slide the old dishwasher out, you'll have to simultaneously work the drain hose back through the hole in the sink cabinet. Keep a rag handy to wipe up the water that'll run out of the line.

Lowering the dishwasher gives you more clearance to slide the dishwasher out. Chances are the leveling feet will be difficult to turn, but a shot of penetrating oil on the threads may make it easier. If you need more clearance, cut the feet off with a hacksaw blade and turn the screw out. Then be sure to slip cardboard or a rug under them to avoid gouging your floor when you pull out the dishwasher.

Prep the new dishwasher

Take out the new dishwasher according to the instructions on the box. Once it's uncrated, you'll find the manuals and installation instructions inside the dishwasher. Review them before proceeding; they may differ slightly from the details we show.

Tip the dishwasher on its back and attach the 90-degree fitting (**Photo 5**). Don't reuse your old drain hose; the dishwasher will come with a new one. To prevent sink clogs from flooding the dishwasher, be sure to loop the flexible drain line all the way up to the bottom of the countertop (**Photo 6**). Some plumbing codes require a special air gap fitting in the drain line. Call your local plumbing inspector to find out the rules.

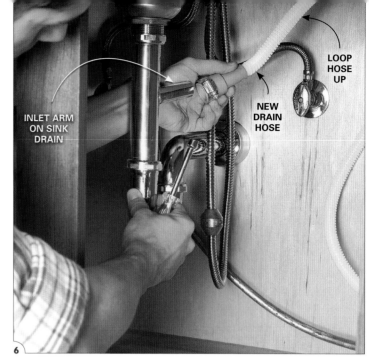

Thread the new drain line into the sink base cabinet. Loop it higher than the inlet arm on the sink drain or garbage disposer. Slip it on and tighten the clamp.

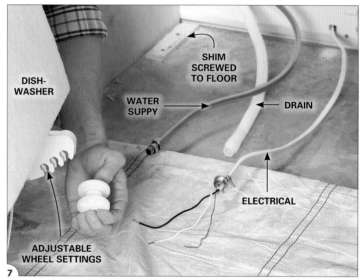

Lay the water supply, drain and electrical lines flat on the floor. Measure the height of the opening, then adjust the wheels and feet according to the manual.

The manual will tell you how to adjust the leveling feet and/or wheels to fit the height of the opening. It's easiest to set these before sliding in the dishwasher. Make minor adjustments after the dishwasher is in. But if your kitchen floor is built up (higher than the area where the dishwasher sits), you'll have to adjust the feet after you slide it into the opening. If your dishwasher is equipped with rear wheels without adjusters in the back, you may have to set shims **(Photo 7)** to raise the back to the height of the finished floor. Tack them to the floor so they don't shake loose when the dishwasher runs.

Slide the dishwasher in and reconnect it

Slide the new dishwasher in **(Photo 8)**, grasping it by the sides to avoid denting the front panel. Set the dishwasher in position according to **Photos 9 and 10**. But don't secure it to the countertop yet. Wait until you make all connections and adjustments.

LEVELING FOOT

8

Grasp the sides of the dishwasher, lift slightly and roll the dishwasher into the opening. Protect the kitchen floor with a tarp or cardboard.

Connecting the copper water line so it doesn't leak can be tricky. The secret is to align it so it slides straight into the threaded part of the elbow (**Photo 11**). If it's cocked to one side, the compression nut won't thread on right and it'll leak. If necessary, turn the elbow on the dishwasher slightly with a wrench to align it, or gently bend copper lines about 8 to 12 in. from the end.

With the supply line, the electrical cable and drain connected, turn the power and water back on and check for leaks. Recheck the positioning, then screw the dishwasher to the countertop (some screw to the cabinet sides). If your countertop is a synthetic material or stone, and the old holes don't line up, follow the directions listed in the manual.

Slide the dishwasher back until it's flush to the cabinets. Positioning may vary slightly according to dishwasher styles and the style of your cabinets.

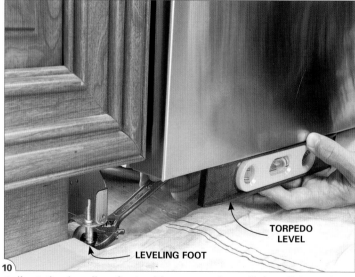

Adjust the leveling feet with a wrench until the dishwasher is level (side to side) and plumb (up and down).

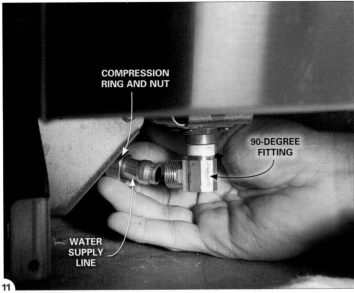

11

Align the water supply line so it slides straight into the 90-degree fitting. Thread on the compression nut (no Teflon tape needed) and tighten with a wrench.

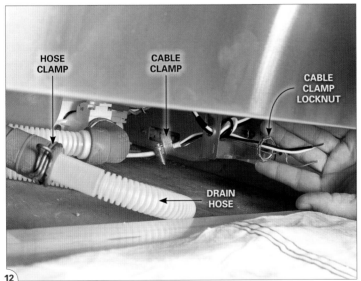

12

Clamp the drain hose to the dishwasher. Then clamp the electrical wires and connect them. Finally, screw the dishwasher to the countertop bottom.

Replace a base cabinet bottom

Let's face it—it's easy to get water on the floor of your sink base cabinet. We'll never understand why cabinetmakers use particleboard for the base, but they do. And once it starts swelling, your only option is to replace it. But you don't have to cut out the entire bottom. Here's an easier way to install a new sink base bottom.

Remove the drain lines (and garbage disposer, if there is one) to get maneuvering room. Then trace a cutting line about 3 in. in from all four edges.

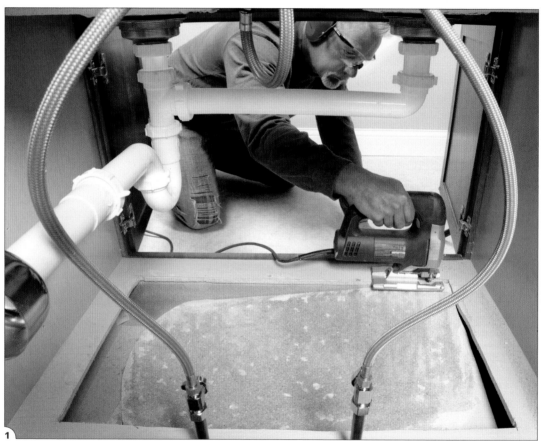

1

Remove the middle section. Drill a 3/4-in. hole in each corner of the traced cutout line. Then run your jigsaw along the line. Remove the old, swollen floor.

Then cut out the middle section of the swollen sink base with a jigsaw (**Photo 1**). Next, cut a piece of 1/2-in. plywood to the interior size of the sink base. Cut slots for the water supply tubes. Then seal the edges and face of the plywood with urethane varnish. Then install the new plywood floor and fasten it to the old floor (**Photo 2**). Caulk around the edges and pipes to prevent water from seeping under the new floor. Then reattach the P-trap and garbage disposer.

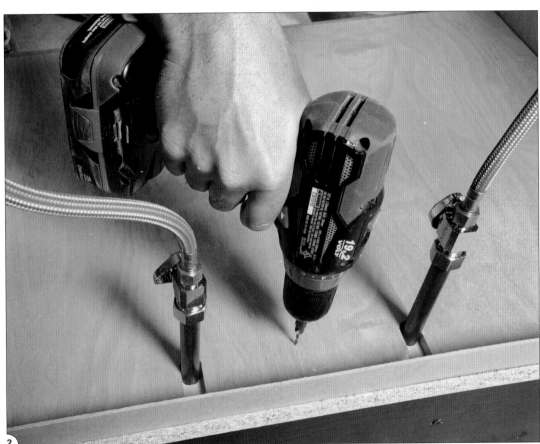

2

Drop in the new floor and screw it into place. Predrill holes around the perimeter using a countersink bit. Then install brass-colored drywall screws.

Replace a vacuum belt

When your vacuum starts to lose cleaning power, requiring multiple passes to get an area clean, or the self-propulsion loses its zip, chances are you need to change the vacuum agitator belt. After only a few months of use, most vacuum belts stretch out enough to slip, causing the agitator to spin more slowly.

Replacing the belt is quick and inexpensive. New belts are available online and at stores that sell vacuums. Belts come in numerous brands and sizes, so bring the old one to the store for a guaranteed match.

Fifteen minutes, two screwdrivers and a new belt are all you'll typically need to complete the job. **Photo 1** shows how to access the old belt. The cover on your vacuum may be held on by other arrangements of clips and screws.

After removing the cover, install the new belt as shown in **Photos 2 and 3**. Once the new belt's on and the agitator's back in place, turn the agitator by hand to make sure the belt spins smoothly, without rubbing or binding. Reassemble the bottom cover and test-run the machine.

1. Unplug the vacuum and turn it over, exposing the underside. Back out the casing screws that secure the bottom cover. Release the attachment clips with a flat-blade screwdriver and lift off the cover.

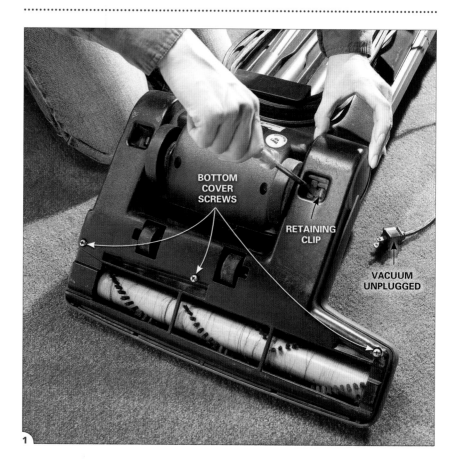

BOTTOM COVER SCREWS

RETAINING CLIP

VACUUM UNPLUGGED

1

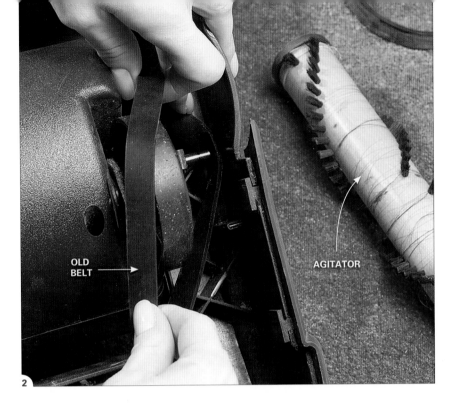

OLD BELT

AGITATOR

2. Pry out the agitator with a flat-blade screwdriver. Slide the old belt off the agitator pulley and motor drive shaft and slide the new belt on the motor drive shaft.

3. Slide the new belt onto the agitator. Replace the agitator, making sure the end caps are properly seated. Spin it with your hand to make sure it doesn't bind, and then replace the cover.

HOLD DOWN

AGITATOR

END CAP

NEW BELT

MOTOR DRIVE SHAFT

Replace a section of split rail fence

Split rail fences are sturdy and long lasting, but occasionally pieces need to be replaced because they're broken or rotted. Rails and posts are available in stock or can be ordered at lumberyards and home centers.

To remove a rail, first mark the bottom of one of the posts with masking tape so you can return it to the proper depth. Dig out the post **(Photo 1)**.

Pull out the damaged rail **(Photo 2)**, then set the new piece into the slots and lower the post back into the hole **(Photo 3)**. Hold the post at the right height and line it up with the other posts as you pack the soil down.

1. Dig to the bottom of one side of the post that holds the rotted rail.

ROTTED RAIL

2. Lift the post out of the ground and remove the old rail.

3. With the new rail in place, set the post back into the hole and tamp the dirt back in around it.

TAPE TO MARK GRADE

NEW RAIL

TAMP DIRT WITH 2x4

PROFESSIONAL
COST: $ 400

YOUR COST: $200

**SAVINGS:
$200**

COMPLEXITY
Moderate

TOOLS
Shovel

Circular saw with
   diamond blade or
   angle grinder

Sledgehammer

Mattock

Screwdriver

Handsaw or recip
   saw

Tape measure

Hand tamper

Drill

Garden hose

Bucket

Small concrete mixer
   (optional)

Wood or magnesium
   float

Edger

Broom

Groover

MATERIALS
2x4s

Stakes

Screws

Masonry nails

Expansion joint
   material

Spray lubricant

Rebar

Bagged concrete mix

Replace a section of sidewalk

Concrete work is hard labor. But for small jobs, you can do it yourself—and for about one-third of what it would cost to hire a pro.

   This sidewalk is a typical example. Experience with concrete isn't necessary, but you will need tool know-how and a strong back. You can follow the steps here and find much more info at familyhandyman.com. Just search for "concrete."

Before

After

What happened? This sidewalk is more than 80 years old and still in good shape—mostly. So what went wrong with this section? Most likely, it was excess water: The builders added too much water to the mix or misted the surface to make troweling easier. Or maybe rain came before the concrete cured. Any of these circumstances makes concrete weak, porous and destined to disintegrate.

Expect a mismatch. New concrete looks very different from older concrete. The match improves with time, but that can mean years. One solution is to replace the entire sidewalk. Another approach—much easier—is to coat the whole sidewalk with a resurfacer. For an overview of that job, search for "resurface sidewalk" at familyhandyman.com.

1

1. **Dig ditches** Trench along both sides of the walk at least 6 in. wide and 6 in. deep. These trenches will allow you to set up forms later.

2. **Cut a crack stop.** When you break up the bad section, a cut that's at least 1-1/4 in. deep will prevent cracks from spreading to the good section. An existing groove in the concrete is usually the best place to cut. Cut with a diamond blade in a circular saw or an angle grinder.

CAUTION
Use your blade guard.

2

3. **Bust up the bad section.** A small section of sidewalk usually doesn't require a jackhammer rental; try a sledgehammer first. A mattock is perfect for prying up broken concrete. Remove the chunks. For more concrete-busting tips, search for "concrete demolition" at familyhandyman.com.

MATTOCK →

3

FORM

4. **Place the forms.** Select straight 2x4s for the forms and drive stakes every 24 in. Position the forms even with the adjoining sections of sidewalk, then drive screws through the stakes into the forms. The forms should feel rock-solid. If not, add stakes.

5. **Trim off the stakes.** Cut the stakes flush with the forms with a handsaw or recip saw. Then span the forms with a 2x4 and slide it along the length of the forms. It should slide smoothly without hitting obstructions.

6. **Prepare the base.** Set a 2x4 across the forms and measure to the soil or gravel below in several spots. Your goal is a 4-in.-deep space for concrete. You may need to add or remove material. Then compact the base with a hand tamper.

7. **Add expansion joints.** Tack expansion joint material to the existing concrete with 1-in. masonry nails. You can get a 50-ft. roll of expansion joint at home centers.

TAMPER

6

EXPANSION JOINT

7

SPRAY LUBRICANT

8. **Oil the forms.** A "release agent" allows for easy form removal after the concrete has cured. Spray lubricant is fast, but you can use a rag to wipe on any oil.

9. **Add rebar.** Rebar isn't essential for sidewalks, but it adds strength and longevity. The 3/8-in. rebar and support "chairs" shown cost less than $20. "Pin" the new concrete to the old: Drill 3-in.-deep holes into the old concrete, insert 16-in. sections of rebar and tie the rebar frame to the pins (**Photo 10**).

CHAIR ⟶

REBAR
↓

10. **Wet the base.** Dry soil or gravel can absorb water and cause concrete to dry out quickly, before it has time to fully cure. Give the base a good dousing, but not enough to create puddles.

11. **Make a measuring bucket.** A strong, workable concrete mix contains just the right amount of water; follow the instructions on the bag. Measure the water into a bucket and mark that level on the bucket.

12. **Mix and dump.** Consider renting a small concrete mixer. Aside from saving you some hard labor, it lets you mix faster, so all your concrete will be at the same stage in the curing process. And that allows for a more consistent finish.

pro tips!

➤ Get tips and how-to help for any concrete project at familyhandyman.com. Just search for "concrete."

REBAR TIED TO "PIN"

10

11

WATER LEVEL

12

SCREED
BOARD

13

FLOAT

14

13. **Screed it flat.** Drag a
2x4 screed board over the
forms as you add concrete
and fill in any low spots.
When the form is evenly
filled, round up a helper for
the final screed. With each
of you holding one side
of the screed board and
making a sawing motion,
screed off the entire length
of the fresh concrete.

14. **Float the concrete.**
Immediately after the
final screed, smooth the
concrete with a wood or
magnesium float. Don't
worry about small ridges
left by the float; broom-
ing the surface will erase
them.

15. **Broom the surface.**
Drag a broom lightly across the concrete to create a nonslip surface. The time to do this is typically 30 minutes after floating, but that will vary a little depending on the temperature and humidity.

16. **Edge the perimeter.**
An edger forms a rounded edge, which looks good and is less likely to chip off. This can be done before or after you broom the surface.

15

EDGER
16

GROOVER

17

17. Groove the surface.
A groover cuts a "control joint," which encourages any cracking to occur in the joint, rather than randomly. Typically, control joints are spaced 5 to 8 ft. apart.

pro tips!

Tips for a smooth, successful project

➤ Once you add water to concrete mix, the clock starts ticking. So the most important step in any concrete work is preparation. Mentally run through the entire job, make a list and be absolutely certain you have all your tools and materials ready to go.

➤ To determine how many bags of concrete mix you need, search online for "bagged concrete calculator." Buy a couple extra bags. Running out can lead to disaster.

➤ Consider renting a mixer or calling in a ready-mix truck. If you need more than 15 bags, rent a mixer. If you need more than 30 bags, order ready-mix.

➤ Whether you're mixing by hand or using a mixer, it's best to have a helper so you can get the final batch mixed before the first batch becomes too stiff to work with.

➤ A couple hours after finishing the concrete, cover it with painter's plastic for a few days. Concrete that stays wet longer grows stronger.

➤ Wait overnight (or longer) before you remove the forms.

Chapter 4

Install It

Install grab bars

Grab bars aren't just safety devices for hospitals and public restrooms. In your own home, a strategically placed and solidly anchored grab bar can mean the difference between a relaxing bath and a trip to the emergency room.

In your bathtub or shower, grab bars provide extra security for that first slippery step. Here, we'll show you where to position grab bars and how to anchor them so they're rock-solid.

If you've mounted towel bars or other hardware around the house, you'll have no trouble installing grab bars. It shouldn't take more than a few hours. You'll only need a hammer, a level, a drill and a few special drill bits. A stud sensor is optional.

Your grab bars will be rock-solid if you anchor them to the studs

If you're mounting your grab bars to standard wood-framed walls, first you'll have to precisely locate the vertical framing members called studs (**Photos 1 and 2**). Most grab bars have three screw holes in each mounting flange, but you'll only be able to anchor two of the three screws into a typical 1-1/2-in.-wide stud. Use a plastic anchor for the third screw. As long as these screws penetrate at least an inch into sound wood, the grab bar will meet or exceed the 250-lb. load rating required by the government for public buildings. More important, it will be plenty strong to support you even in a fall. On pp. 98, 99 and 101, we show you how to

STUD
SENSOR

1

Find the studs near your proposed grab bar location using a stud sensor or one of the techniques mentioned in the story. Make a light pencil mark at the center of each stud.

mount grab bars to fiberglass tubs and showers, hollow walls and concrete.

Studs are easy to find in walls with only a single layer of drywall over the framing. Rap on the wall with your knuckle until the sound changes from hollow to a dull thud, or use a stud sensor **(Photo 1)**. Thicker wall coverings like plaster present a greater challenge. Here are a few tips:

> ➤ Remove the access hatch behind the tub drain and peer behind the tub with a flashlight to look for studs.

> ➤ Go to the room or closet behind the long tub wall and look for clues to stud locations like nails in the baseboard. Then measure from a reference point you can identify when you go back into the bathroom.

> ➤ More hints for finding studs can be found by searching for "finding studs" at familyhandyman.com.

When you've located what you believe to be the center of the studs, confirm the stud locations and find both edges by probing with a nail **(Photo 2)**. If wall tile extends to the ceiling, drill 1/8-in. holes with a glass-and-tile or masonry bit in a horizontal grout line instead. Patch the holes later with matching grout or caulk.

Mark the studs and grab bar mounting holes **(Photo 4)**. Then drill a 1/8-in. hole at one of the marks located over a stud. If you

continued on p. 98

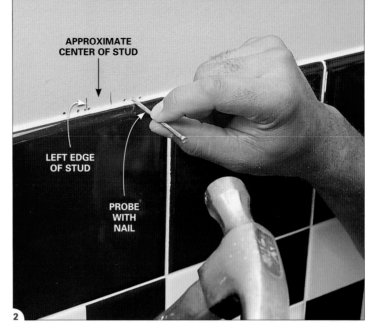

Find the edges of the studs by probing with a finish nail. Make a series of holes in an inconspicuous location, like directly above the tile, and mark both edges of the studs.

Extend the stud marks down to the grab bar location with a level. Place a strip of 1-1/2 in. masking tape on the tile to indicate the studs.

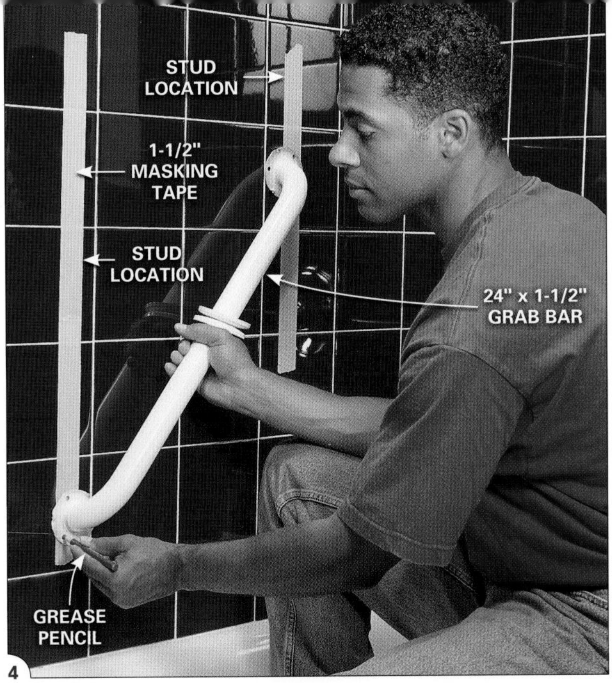
STUD
LOCATION
1-1/2"
MASKING
TAPE
STUD
LOCATION
24" x 1-1/2"
GRAB BAR
GREASE
PENCIL
4

Position the grab bar (see "Positioning Your Grab Bars," right) so that at least two of the screw holes align with the studs. Then mark each hole with a grease pencil.

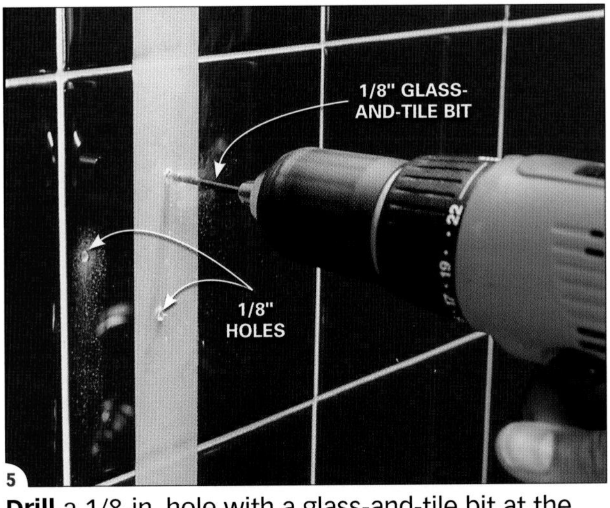
1/8" GLASS-
AND-TILE BIT
1/8"
HOLES
5

Drill a 1/8-in. hole with a glass-and-tile bit at the mark closest to the center of each stud to confirm the stud location. If you hit solid wood, drill the remaining holes. If not, poke a piece of bent wire through the hole and probe until you feel the stud. Reposition the grab bar and mark the holes over the new stud position.

Positioning your grab bars

Even a solidly anchored grab bar is useless if it's in the wrong place. Which location is best depends on the particular situation. If you're installing the bars for a person with a disability or injury, have this person help you decide which location will be most helpful. A physical therapist or an occupational therapist also can help with this decision. For solid anchoring, stud locations are critical too. (Later we'll tell you what to do if studs aren't available.)

Here are guidelines for placing the bars:

- Place an 18-in. to 24-in. long bar vertically at the tub edge **(Photo 8)** to assist in getting in and out of the tub. The bottom of the bar should be 32 to 38 in. above the floor. Position the bar so it can be anchored to a wall stud.
- Mount a bar at an angle between two wall studs on the long back wall of the tub **(Photo 7)**. The bottom of the bar should be about 6 to 10 in. above the top of the tub. For studs 16 in. apart, a 24-in. long bar provides a nice angle. A person can use this grab bar to help lower themself and get up again. If this bar will be used primarily by a person sitting in a bath chair, raise the bottom to about 18 in. above the tub.
- Mount a bar horizontally about 36 in. to 38 in. above the bottom of the tub as a convenient handhold while showering.

continued from p. 96

miss the stud, adjust the grab bar location accordingly and drill new holes. In most cases, the unused hole will be covered by the mounting plate on the grab bar.

Complete the grab bar installation as shown in **Photos 6 and 7**. Use a 1/4-in. glass-and-tile or masonry bit to enlarge the holes. Then use a 5/32-in. wood bit to drill pilot holes into the stud. This will make driving the screws easier.

Insert a plastic anchor in the holes in the tile that miss the stud. Then screw the bar to the wall with No. 10 or 12 stainless steel panhead screws. Make sure the screws penetrate the studs at least 1 in. In most cases, 2-in. screws are long enough.

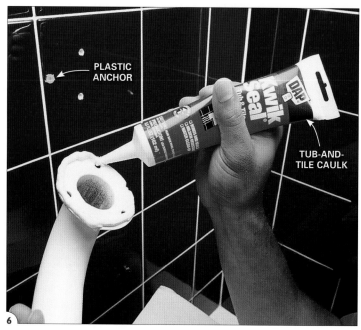

PLASTIC ANCHOR

TUB-AND-TILE CAULK

6 Caulk the back of the grab bar mounting flange with tub-and-tile adhesive or silicone caulk.

Special toggle bolt for hollow walls

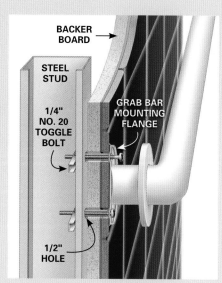

BACKER BOARD

STEEL STUD

1/4" NO. 20 TOGGLE BOLT

GRAB BAR MOUNTING FLANGE

1/2" HOLE

Toggler brand toggle bolts work great for hollow walls or steel studs. If you simply can't mount your grab bar to a stud or solid wood backing, then these Toggler brand 1/4-in. toggle bolts are the thing to use. Follow the instructions on the package to mount the toggle. Then use a 2-in. x 1/4-in. x No. 20 stainless steel machine screw to attach the grab bar to the toggle anchor. Use the same method to mount grab bars to steel studs.

1/4" TOGGLE BOLT

1/4" NO. 20 STAINLESS STEEL MACHINE SCREW

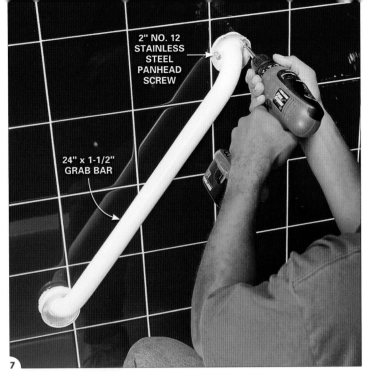

2" NO. 12 STAINLESS STEEL PANHEAD SCREW

24" x 1-1/2" GRAB BAR

7

Screw the grab bar to the wall with the No. 10 or 12 stainless steel panhead screws supplied with the grab bar. They should penetrate the stud at least 1 in.

If you simply can't anchor to a stud, you have a few options. The best alternative is to secure wood blocking between the studs. However, this requires opening a small hole in the wall and patching it after the blocking is screwed into place. If possible, work from the backside of the tub wall, where you're not hindered by ceramic tile or other tub finishes. If you're lucky, you'll have a closet or storage area where the wall patch doesn't have to be perfect.

As a last resort, use toggle bolts or WingIts to mount the grab bar to the hollow part of the wall. The plaster, mortar or tile backer must be dry and solid and at least 5/8 in. thick.

Special anchor for fiberglass enclosures

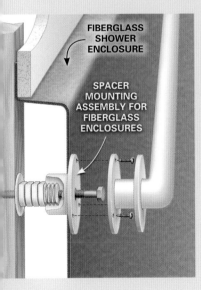

FIBERGLASS SHOWER ENCLOSURE

SPACER MOUNTING ASSEMBLY FOR FIBERGLASS ENCLOSURES

The Solid Mount solves the fiberglass shower problem. Fiberglass tub and shower enclosures present a unique challenge. You must mount the grab bar to a stud, but the space between the stud and fiberglass must also be filled with something, or the fiberglass will bend as you tighten the mounting screws. The Solid Mount, is available at amazon.com.

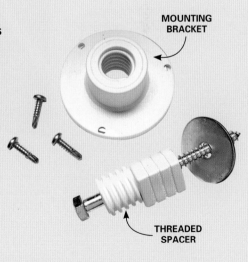

MOUNTING BRACKET

THREADED SPACER

You're not done until you do the yank test

Give the bars a good solid yank to test their holding power (**Photo 8**). With a helper standing by in case the bar comes loose, pull with all your strength. Now's the time to make sure the bar will hold up when it's really needed.

While you're at it, consider installing grab bars in other key locations. A vertical or angled bar mounted on the wall to the side of the toilet or a vertical bar installed on the side wall in front of the toilet helps getting up or down. The expert we talked to recommended mounting a vertical bar beside the entry door from an attached garage. Usually there isn't a handrail, and negotiating two or three steps with a bag of groceries under your arm is a lot easier and safer with a grab bar to hang on to. Look around and you'll find other spots where grab bars would make everyday tasks safer and easier.

18" x 1-1/2" GRAB BAR

8

Attach a vertical grab bar near the tub edge, following the procedures shown in **Photos 1–7**. The bottom of the bar should be about 32 in. to 38 in. above the floor. Yank both grab bars to test for a strong connection.

Buying grab bars

Grab bars are specially manufactured to hold at least 250 lbs. when properly secured. Towel bars and other light-duty bars are not strong enough.

Most bars are stainless steel to resist corrosion, but you can also find them with a painted finish in a variety of colors. We purchased our 1-1/2 in. dia. white grab bars at a home center. The 18-in. bar cost about $40; the 24-in. bar about $50. Thinner bars are available, but a standard 1-1/2 in. dia. bar like we're using is just right for most people's grip. Some bars feature added texture to reduce slipping. Here are a few guidelines for selecting grab bars:

- ➤ Purchase an 18-in. or longer bar to mount vertically at the tub edge.
- ➤ Before you buy a bar to mount at an angle or horizontally on the long tub wall (**Photos 1 and 2**), locate the studs. Then buy a bar that reaches from one stud to the other, usually 32 in. long for a horizontal bar and 24 in. long for an angled bar.
- ➤ Buy standard 1-1/2 in. dia. grab bars for most situations. Thinner bars look more like towel bars and may not be strong enough for heavy use.
- ➤ Avoid grab bars that leave more than a 1-1/2 in. space between the bar and the wall unless there is a specific reason for using one. A person's arm could slip into the extra-wide space and become trapped or break during a fall.
- ➤ Ask a physical therapist or an occupational therapist to help select the right bars if you're installing the grab bars for a person with special needs.

Home centers keep a variety of grab bars in stock, and you will find many sources online.

The best way to anchor grab bars to concrete

Plastic plug anchors hold screws tight in masonry or concrete. Anchor grab bars to concrete, concrete block or brick with 1/4-in. x 1-1/2 in. plastic plug anchors and No. 12 stainless steel panhead screws. Drill a 1/4-in. hole with a masonry bit (you may need a hammer drill for concrete or hard brick). Push the sleeve into the hole and drive in the screw.

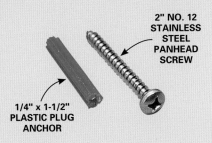

2" NO. 12 STAINLESS STEEL PANHEAD SCREW

1/4" x 1-1/2" PLASTIC PLUG ANCHOR

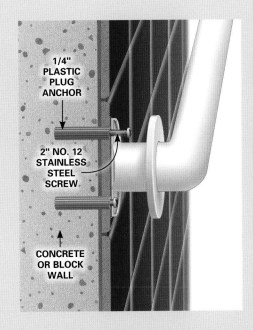

1/4" PLASTIC PLUG ANCHOR

2" NO. 12 STAINLESS STEEL SCREW

CONCRETE OR BLOCK WALL

Install carpet squares

PROFESSIONAL COST: $500

YOUR COST: $300 (including carpet)

SAVINGS: $200

COMPLEXITY
Simple

TOOLS
Chalk line
Carpenter's square
Tape measure
Carpet knife

MATERIALS
Carpet squares
Graph paper
Stiff paper for templates

If you think installing new carpet is time consuming and complicated, think again. Modular carpet, aka carpet squares, is one of the easiest floor coverings to install. You simply lay the squares on the floor; adhesive strips and the carpet's heavy backing hold them in place. You can finish most rooms in a day, if not an afternoon. And you can use it anywhere. You can add whimsy to a kids' playroom or create an elegant look in a formal dining room.

Or, if you don't need wall-to-wall carpet, these squares make great area rugs. Cleaning, replacing or swapping squares is easy too. They just pull right up—even after they're adhered. You can clean off stained squares in the sink or replace them. Is that kid-friendly or what?

Modular carpet is slightly more expensive than most conventional carpets. The squares cost up to $18 per sq. ft., with most in the $1.50 to $9 per sq. ft. range, but a carpet pad isn't required and you save by installing it yourself.

Here we'll show you how to install the carpet and cut it to fit around obstacles such as doorjambs. Installation is nearly goof-proof—you can easily pull up misaligned squares and reposition them. And you won't need any specialty tools. A tape measure and chalk line to snap your baselines and a carpenter's square and utility knife to cut the squares will get the job done.

Plan your pattern and order the carpet

With practically unlimited carpet options, the hardest part may be choosing a design. You'll have to select the brand you want before you start, since the brands have different sizes of squares. Then sketch the room to scale and use colored pencils or markers to draw in the squares **(Photo 1)**.

Arrange your layout to avoid leaving narrow strips along the walls. They call attention to any wall not perfectly square. If possible, allow at least 4-in.-wide sections of carpet along each wall. Your final design will tell you how many squares of each color you'll need.

Determine the room's square footage by multiplying the length by the width (round up measurements to the nearest foot). For irregular-shaped rooms, divide the floor into individual sections, calculate the square footage of each, then add them together. Order

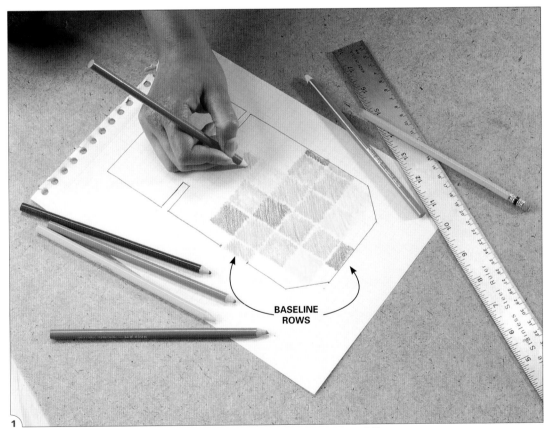

BASELINE ROWS

1 Draw the room to scale on graph paper to experiment with different designs. Mark your baseline rows on the sketch.

the carpet, adding an extra 10 percent for waste.

Assess your existing floor

You can lay carpet squares directly over concrete, plywood and OSB or particleboard subfloors, as well as over vinyl, tile, laminate and some hardwood finished floors. One caution: The backing may eventually discolor some wood floors. If you later decide to remove the carpet, you'll have to refinish the wood.

Conduct a moisture test (kits available for $7 at home centers) before carpeting a concrete floor. If the moisture content is too high, you can always seal the concrete, then install the carpet. Let new concrete cure for at least 90 days first. Any wood subfloor or existing floor has to be solid, dry and securely fastened. Screw down any loose areas of floor and replace any water-damaged sections. This is also an ideal time to find and fix any floor squeaks.

2

Clean the floor, then snap chalk lines parallel to the walls to create perpendicular baselines.

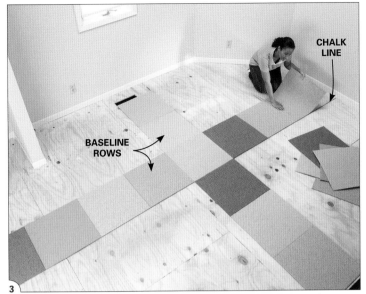

Labels on image:
- CHALK LINE
- BASELINE ROWS

3

Lay carpet squares along both baselines, starting at the center. Remove the protective film, butt the squares tightly and adhere them to the floor.

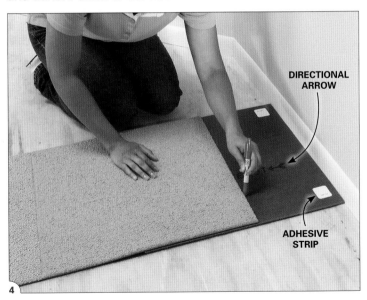

- DIRECTIONAL ARROW
- ADHESIVE STRIP

4

Place the last carpet square face down against the wall and under the previous square. Mark it, cut it to size with a carpet knife and install it.

Install the baseline rows

Prepare the floor by sweeping or vacuuming up all dust and grit. Then, using your sketch as a guide, pick the spot for the base rows (**Photo 2**). Keep them as close to the center of the room as possible, since they guide the rest of the installation.

Measure and snap your perpendicular baselines for those rows (**Photo 2**). Lay carpet squares (without adhesive) along both baselines to test the layout. If you end up with gaps less than 4 in. next to walls, shift the layout and snap new baselines.

To install the squares, start where the baselines intersect and work outward (**Photo 3**). Keep the directional arrows (**Photo 4**) on the back of the squares pointing in the same direction.

Peel the film off the adhesive strips and butt each square tightly against the preceding one. Don't adhere the last full square until you cut the final square to size (**Photo 4**). After you cut the square, add two adhesive strips so there's one in all four corners. Extra strips come in the box. Then adhere the final pieces.

You only have to adhere the baseline rows and the squares on both sides of the baselines and along the perimeter of the room. The others stay put thanks to their heavy backing. (No, they don't pop out when you're vacuuming!)

A utility knife works OK for cutting the squares, but we prefer the type of carpet knife shown below because it's a bit more accurate. Use a sharp blade and make several shallow passes. The backing allows for a crisp cut that won't unravel. Cut the squares on a smooth surface, like hardboard. Avoid cutting on a plywood subfloor since the wood grain can pull the blade off line.

Fill in the quadrants

With the base rows in place, start back at the center and fill in the quadrants using a "step" pattern **(Photo 5)**. Simply press each square snugly against adjacent squares, keeping carpet strands out of the joints.

You can easily change out squares for a more pleasing design, even if they're adhered. If the adhesive residue remains, remove it with rubbing alcohol.

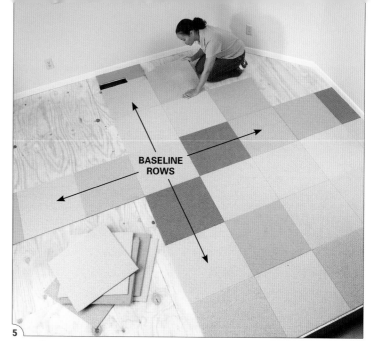

BASELINE ROWS

5

Install carpet squares in each quadrant, starting at the center and moving outward. Adhere only the squares along the baselines and walls.

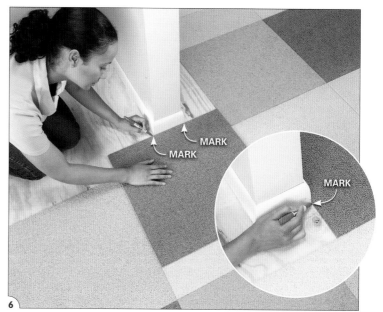

MARK
MARK
MARK

6

Place a carpet square right side up against an archway wall, aligning it with installed squares. Mark the wall location on the edges of the carpet.

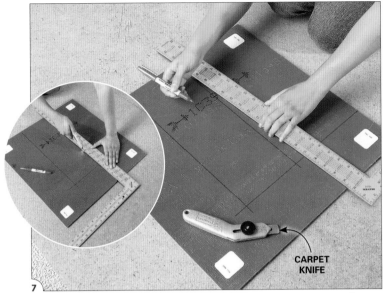

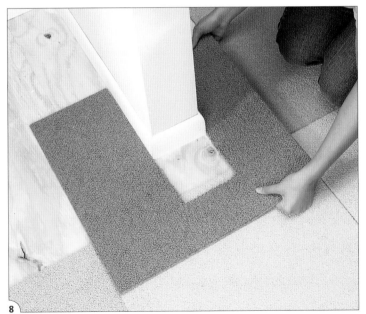

CARPET KNIFE

7

Flip the square over and use a marker and a carpenter's square to draw the wall shape from the marks you just made. Cut out the opening **(inset photo)**.

Fitting around doorjambs and corners

Cutting carpet to fit around outside corners, archway walls and doorjambs is the most challenging part of the job. Start by setting a square against the face of the archway wall, overlapping and aligned with the previously installed square **(Photo 6)**. Mark the carpet on each side of the wall, then place the same square against the side of the wall and mark it **(Photo 6 inset)**.

Using the marks, outline your cut with your carpenter's square as a guide **(Photo 7)**. It's best to slightly undercut the mark, then fine-tune as needed for a tight fit. This same method works for marking and notching squares to fit around corners.

CARPET KNIFE

8

Install the square against the archway wall. Fine-tune the cut, if necessary, so the square fits snug.

To fit carpet around odd-shaped obstacles, such as doorjambs with angular trim, first make a paper template. You'll need to make several measurements, transfer them to paper, then cut out the opening. It'll probably take several tries before you get a good fit. Once the template fits, trace the outline onto the back of a carpet square and cut it **(Photo 9)**.

Don't worry if the cut isn't perfect and you end up with a gap—carpet squares are very forgiving! Just cut a small sliver of carpet from a scrap piece and tuck it snugly into the gap **(Photo 10)**.

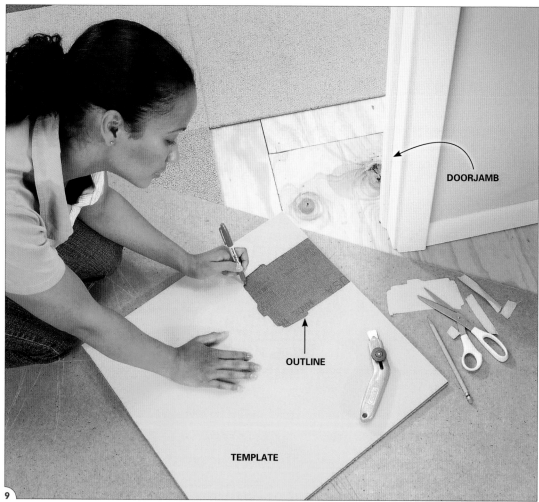

DOORJAMB

OUTLINE

TEMPLATE

9

Make a full-size template for doorjambs with complicated trim and doorstops. Transfer the outline onto a carpet square, then cut the square.

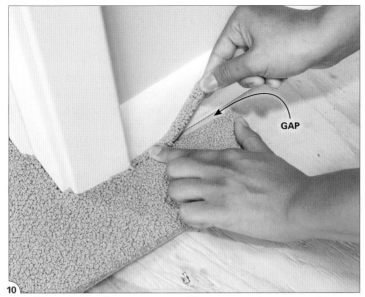

Since the carpet won't unravel, threshold strips aren't required. Instead, you can simply butt against the flooring in the next room or the existing threshold (**Photo 11**).

After all of the squares are installed, vacuum the floor. It's inevitable that something will eventually spill on the floor, but carpet squares are easy to clean. If the spill doesn't wipe up, remove the square and rinse it with water in the sink. Let it dry and replace it in the floor. For squares with permanent stains, just replace the old square with a new one.

10 Cut filler pieces from scrap to fill any gaps between the walls and squares. Wedge the pieces into place, then smooth them with your hand.

11 Butt the carpet against the flooring in adjacent rooms, or overlap the edge of the adjoining floor.

PROFESSIONAL
COST: $1,000

YOUR COST: $50

**SAVINGS:
$950**

COMPLEXITY
Moderate

TOOLS
Reciprocating saw

Tape measure

Hammer

MATERIALS
AC unit

Nails

2x4s

Install air conditioning in your garage

Working on a car or doing a project in a sweltering garage is no fun. The heat and humidity slow you down, make you grumpy and increase your frustration. Air-conditioning your garage solves those problems and doesn't cost a fortune. You can buy a TTW (through-the-wall) unit for about $700. Window units cost a bit less, so consider going that route if you have a suitable window. Window and TTW units are the same except for installation. A window unit comes with hardware and sealing gear for mounting it in a window, while a TTW unit requires a separate sleeve that fits into a wall opening that you frame into the wall.

If you start the installation in the morning, you'll be enjoying cold air by mid-afternoon. A ceiling fan helps circulate the air and eliminate hot spots, but if the A/C unit keeps you cool enough, you can skip the fan. We'll show you how to pick the right size unit for your garage and how to install it in the wall.

Consider insulating first

If you plan to use your garage A/C only occasionally, you don't have to install insulation. It'll just take longer to lower the temperature to a comfortable level and the A/C compressor will run for longer periods, costing you more in electric bills. However, you can dramatically speed up the cool-down time and increase cooling effectiveness by hanging drywall on the ceiling. That reduces the size of the area to be cooled and helps the cool air circulate. Install a vapor barrier first, in case you decide to add attic insulation later on. But if you plan to frequently use the garage A/C, it's well worth insulating and finishing the entire space.

Cut the stud. Cut through the center stud, leaving a space 3 in. taller than the rough opening height of the A/C sleeve to allow room for the top and bottom plates. Knock the cut piece sideways to break it loose from the sheathing and siding nails.

Then size the A/C unit

Measure the area of your garage (length times width) to determine the total square footage, then consult the chart on p. 115 . Apply the adjusting factors at the bottom of the chart. Then shop around for the best price on the A/C unit and a matching through-the-wall sleeve (an additional $100 to the cost of a window unit).

Pick a location and cut the opening

A/C units have weak circulating fans, so don't locate one on the end wall of a large, rectangular garage. Instead, locate it in the middle of the longest wall and aim the airflow toward the garage door. If you're installing a window unit and it's located on the end wall of a rectangular

2

Frame the sleeve opening. Nail top and bottom plates to the center and adjacent studs. Then add a short jack stud to frame the opening to the proper width.

garage, plan to install circulating fans to help move the cold air to the other end.

Next, check the sleeve installation instructions for the rough opening size. Some manufacturers want a 1-in. clearance on the sides and top of the sleeve. Plus, the distance from the ceiling is critical. Don't place the opening directly below the top wall plate. That'll result in rapid compressor cycling and inefficient cooling. Locate the top of the sleeve opening about 24 in. down from the ceiling (or as shown in the sleeve installation instructions). Then remove drywall (if any) in that location to expose the studs. Cut the center stud to allow for the thickness of the new top and sill plates. The biggest task is reworking the siding. In most cases it's best to remove as much siding as needed before cutting the opening in the sheathing and then to trim and re-side around the opening. Follow the

SHEATHING

3

Cut through sheathing. Test-fit the sleeve before cutting out the sheathing with a reciprocating saw.

manufacturer's instructions to mount and secure the sleeve to the framing.

Run electrical cable to the location and install the receptacle. Most 120-volt units require a dedicated receptacle on either a 15- or 20-amp circuit breaker (no extension cords allowed). A unit sized from 9,000 to 12,000 Btu will typically run on a 20-amp, 120-volt circuit. But you'll have to install a 220-volt circuit for larger units.

OUTLET
ON
DEDICATED
CIRCUIT

4

Install the sleeve. Secure the sleeve brackets (if equipped), install filler strips and secure the sleeve.

A/C sizing for an insulated garage

Typical garage size	Square feet	Btus for TTW or window unit
2-car (18' x 20')	360	9,000
2.5-car (22' x 22')	484	12,000
3-car (20' x 32')	640	14,000

Adjusting factors:
- Buy the next larger size if your garage isn't insulated.
- Add 10 percent if the garage is exposed to direct sunlight.

Add circulation fans

A through-the-wall A/C unit will dump most of its cool air right into the center of the garage, creating hot spots around the sides. To get more uniform cooling, add a ceiling fan to suck hot air from the ceiling corners and blow it down to the floor. Use a floor fan on the opposite side to blow the newly warmed floor air up toward the A/C unit intake.

Other A/C options for your garage

We didn't cover portable A/C units here. They're an option but not a very good one. Portable units use cold air from the room to cool the condensing coil and then exhaust that air to the outdoors. The negative pressure this creates inside the garage draws in an equal amount of hot humid "make-up" air from outside. The portable unit then has to cool that make-up air and the cycle repeats over and over, wasting 30 to 50 percent of the rated capacity of the unit. Overall, portable units don't come close to the efficiency of a window unit or a TTW unit.

If you want the very best cooling option and are willing to dig deep (expect to pay about $4,000), contact an HVAC company and get quotes on a split system. Those are heavy-duty units that can quickly cool your garage and maintain the temperature even under the hottest conditions.

Install a reverse-osmosis water filter

If you buy lots of bottled or filtered water or you're worried about your tap water, a reverse-osmosis water filter can be a good investment. They can provide 10 or more gallons of drinking water a day for $150 to $300, plus $100 to $200 annually for replacement filters.

Reverse-osmosis filters remove many pollutants and chemicals, separating them from the water and then flushing them into the drain line. The purified water is then fed to the storage tank or the spout on the sink. However, reverse-osmosis filters remove the minerals that give water its taste, so try a gallon (available at most supermarkets) before buying a system.

First, hang the filter assembly on the back or side wall of the sink base (or in the basement close to the sink location) at the height specified in the instructions. Turn off both the cold and the hot water shutoffs, and then install (after the cold water shutoff) the tee or saddle valve included with the unit.

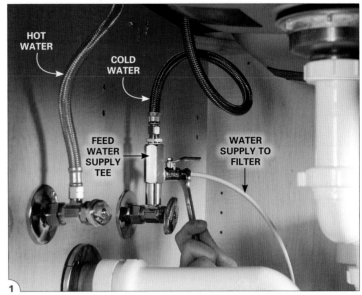

1 Push the plastic supply tube onto the inlet valve, then tighten the nut a half-turn past hand-tight.

2 Feed the water supply line and the two waste lines up through the hole in the sink and through the gasket and faucet base, then attach them.

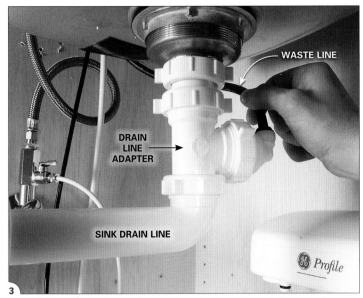

Cut the color-coded water supply line so that it's above the cabinet base and won't get kinked. Fasten the plastic tubing to the supply valve **(Photo 1)**.

Shorten the supply and waste lines to the faucet to eliminate excess tubing, but don't cut the larger black waste line yet. Attach the lines to the fittings on the base of the faucet **(Photo 2)**. The black waste lines feed through the base of the faucet to keep them above possible sink backups, but they have no connection to the supply.

Fasten the faucet to the sink, then install the drain line adapter under the sink basket. Cut the waste line so that it flows downhill with no loops, then push it into the adapter **(Photo 3)**.

Set the storage tank into place and install the final water line. Sterilize and fill the system according to the manufacturer's instructions **(Photo 4)**.

Install the drain line adapter just below the sink and above the discharge from the disposer and/or dishwasher.

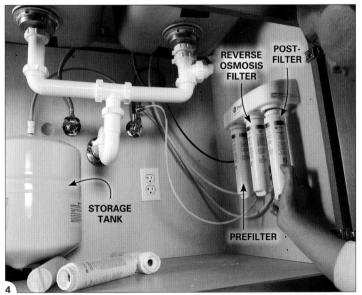

Before using the system, sanitize it and then fill and drain it to rinse it clean. Check all the fittings for leaks.

Install cabinet hardware

There's more to installing kitchen hardware than drilling holes and screwing on knobs and pulls. Whether you're installing hardware on brand new cabinets or replacing the hardware in a 100-year-old kitchen, think before you drill. Cabinets are expensive, and they look a whole lot better without extra holes. We asked Jerome Worm for some tips on how he installs the "jewelry of the kitchen." Use these tips to help your next install go quicker and with fewer mistakes.

Use the door rail as a guide

The location of knobs and pulls isn't written in stone, but there are some "standard practices." One good rule of thumb is to line up a knob with the top of the bottom door rail. If you're installing door pulls, line up the bottom of the pull with the top of the door rail. Always center them on the door stile.

TOP OF RAIL

STILE

RAIL

Temporarily attach the hardware

Ultimately, the person paying for the hardware has the final word on where the knobs and pulls are to be installed. If Jerome's customers don't like his suggestions, he sticks a piece of reusable putty adhesive to the hardware and lets them put it wherever they want. He marks that spot with a pencil and installs the rest of the hardware accordingly. DAP makes a reusable adhesive called BLUESTIK. Buy a package at a home center or hardware store.

ADHESIVE PUTTY

Super-glue the knob

Oblong and rectangular knobs that fasten with a single screw are notorious for twisting over time. Thread sealant will keep a screw from coming loose from the knob, but it won't necessarily stop the knob from twisting. Jerome avoids callbacks by adding a drop of super glue to the back of these types of knobs before he installs them.

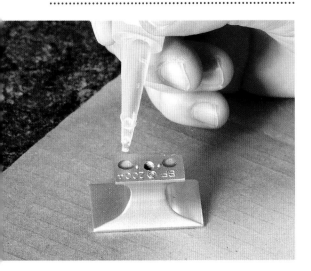

OLD HOLES

BACK PLATE

Hide old holes with back plates

If you're switching from a pull to a knob or you'd prefer to select pulls with a different hole pattern, you can cover the old holes or hide damaged surfaces with back plates. Home centers don't have a huge selection, so consider buying yours from an online source like myknobs.com. You'll find hundreds to choose from.

Templates make the job easier

If you have more than a few knobs or pulls to install, use a template. A template makes the job go faster, increases uniformity and reduces the chance for mistakes. The Liberty Cabinet and Drawer Installation Templates shown cost about $10 at a home center.

   If you install a lot of hardware, buy a pro version like the one used in the photo on p. 118. That's an EZ-JIG EZ1000. It's adjustable and has steel grommets where you insert the drill bit. You can get one for about $55 at hghhardware.com.

TEMPLATE

Make a simple drawer template

If you don't have a template, make one. This simple template consists of two pieces of wood and takes only a few minutes to make. This same template can be used for almost any size door and most hardware sizes.

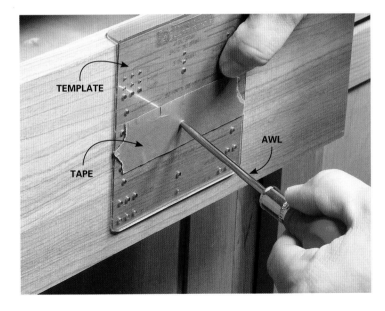

TEMPLATE

TAPE

AWL

Cover unused holes with tape

Store-bought templates and well-used homemade templates have a bunch of holes you won't use on every job. Avoid using the wrong hole by sticking masking tape over the jig, and poking through only the holes you need. Instead of using a pencil to mark the location of the hole on the cabinet, use an awl. That way your drill bit won't skate off in the wrong direction when you drill the hole.

Use thread sealant to keep the screws tight

Every time the screw in a knob works itself loose, you are going to be unhappy. Add a dab of removable thread sealant to every screw you install. Loctite is one brand.

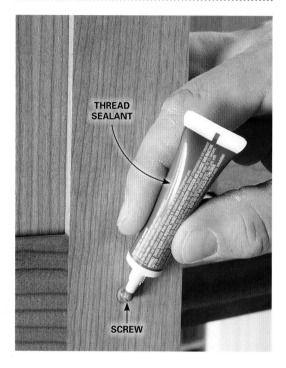

THREAD SEALANT

SCREW

Don't install hardware in front of the sink

The false drawer directly in front of the sink may look naked without any hardware, but it's not very comfortable getting poked by a knob in your midsection every time you lean over the sink.

TWO-SIDED TEMPLATE

Two-sided templates prevent tear-out

If you're having problems with the wood on the back side of the cabinet doors tearing out every time you drill a hole, make a two-sided template. Make sure the spacer wood is close to the same size as the cabinet doors. The tighter the fit, the less chance of tear-out.

Mix putty to match

If back plates won't cover the old holes, use putty to fill them. The wood grain on cabinet doors and fronts usually varies in color, so take one of the doors to a hardware store or home center and buy three different colors of putty. Buy one that matches the darkest grain, one that matches the lightest grain and one halfway between. Use the three to mix a custom color to fill the holes.

HIGHER THAN CENTER

Take old hardware to the store

Not every pull is the same size, and not every cabinet door/drawer is the same thickness. If you have the old hardware with you at the store, you'll be able to tell the size of the pulls you need as well as the length of screws required.

Install hardware higher on the lowest drawer

Most drawer pulls are centered on the drawer fronts, but if the cabinet you're working on has two or three drawers the same size and one larger one at the bottom, install the bottom knob (or pull) higher than the center of that drawer front. Install it so all the knobs on the cabinet are spaced evenly. This configuration is pleasing to the eye—and you don't have to bend over as far to open the bottom drawer.

YOUR COST: $75

SAVINGS: $175

COMPLEXITY
Simple

TOOLS
4 ft. level

Drill bit set

Drill/driver-cordless

Hammer

Magnetic driver
  bit holder

Miter saw

Nail set

Stud finder

Tape measure

MATERIALS
Code-approved
  handrail material

Handrail brackets

2-part, 90-second
  epoxy

4 ft. of 2x4

Masking tape

Nails

Wood glue

Sandpaper

Install a rock-solid handrail

Would your stair rail hold up to three energetic youngsters hanging on it like this? If you're not sure, or if you have stairways with missing rails, now's the time to fix the problem. More accidents happen on stairways than anywhere else in the house, and a strong stair rail goes a long way toward making stairs safer and easier to use.

Here we'll show you how to cut and assemble your rail and how to mount it solidly to the wall framing. The design we chose slightly exceeds the building codes in many regions. We extended the railing beyond both the top and the bottom steps. While this isn't always possible, it allows you to grasp the railing sooner and hold on longer to maintain good balance.

Not including staining or painting, this project will take you less than half a day. It requires only basic carpentry tools, but we recommend using a power miter saw for the angle cuts.

Before you go shopping for your rail, measure from the nosing of the top landing to the floor at the bottom of the stairs and add 2 ft. This is the length of rail material you'll need. You'll find code-approved handrail and the other materials you'll need at lumberyards and home centers. Expect to spend about $10 per linear foot for an oak rail like the one we're using. Pine and poplar rails cost less. In addition to the rail, you'll need handrail brackets (p. 130), a package of two-part, 90-second epoxy, and about 4 ft. of 2x4. Buy enough brackets to install two at the top, one at the bottom and one every 48 in. between the top and the bottom.

STUD LOCATIONS

STUD FINDER

MASKING TAPE

1

Locate the studs in the wall above the stairs. Use a stud finder and mark the locations with strips of 1-1/2 in. masking tape centered about 36 in. above the stairs.

Locate and mark the studs

In order to be safe, stair rails must be anchored securely to the wood framing behind the drywall or plaster. Here are a few tips for locating the studs. Start by inspecting the skirt board to see if you can detect a pattern of nails that may indicate studs. Then use a stud finder to verify the locations. Most studs are 16 in. on center, so once you find one, you can try measuring horizontally to locate the next one. When you find a stud, mark it with a strip of masking tape (**Photo 1**). We used blue tape for photo clarity, but Scotch Safe-Release masking tape would be a better choice to avoid damaging the paint or wallpaper. Mark every stud along the stairs, plus one beyond the top and bottom risers. You'll decide later which ones to use. Studs aren't always where you want them. If no stud is available at the top, use metal toggle anchors to mount the bracket under the short horizontal section of rail. If the wall ends close to the top or bottom step, you won't be able to extend the rail. Instead simply return it to the wall.

In addition to finding the studs, you have to make marks at the top and bottom of the stairway to indicate the height of the rail above the stairs. To meet building code requirements, the rail should be mounted so that the top is 34 to 38 in. above the front edge of the stair nosings.

2

STAIR NOSING

PLUMB MARK

36" ABOVE STAIR NOSING

Plumb up from the front edge of the top stair nosing and stick a piece of tape to the wall. Make a vertical line even with the front of the nosing and a horizontal line at 36 in. Do the same at the bottom tread.

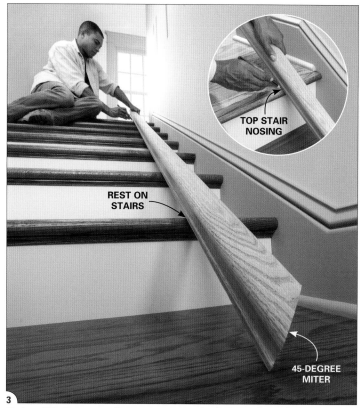

3

REST ON STAIRS

TOP STAIR NOSING

45-DEGREE MITER

Cut a 45-degree miter on one end of the rail and rest this end on the floor. With the rail resting on the front of the stair treads, mark where the rail contacts the top stair nosing (see **inset photo**).

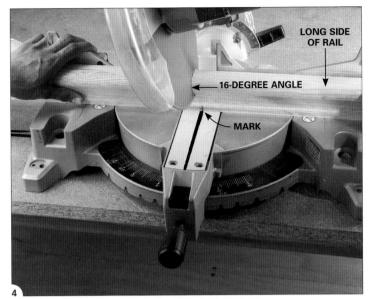

LONG SIDE OF RAIL

16-DEGREE ANGLE

MARK

4 Test the fit of the rail joint. Adjust the cutting angle and recut both pieces until the joint is tight. Then cut a 45-degree miter on the other end of the short piece, allowing enough length to reach the next stud.

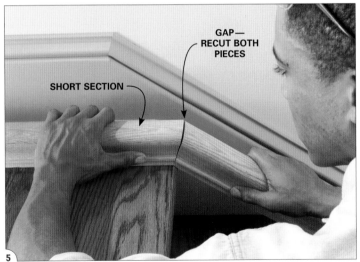

GAP— RECUT BOTH PIECES

SHORT SECTION

5 Mix 90-second epoxy for 30 seconds, apply a thin layer to the end of both rail sections, and press and hold the pieces together for one minute until the epoxy starts to set. Carefully remove the protective masking tape after about five minutes. Let the epoxy harden for at least two hours.

We chose 36 in. **Photo 2** shows how to find this point at the top of the stair. Repeat the process on the bottom step. Later you'll align the top of the rail with these marks and locate the rail brackets **(Photo 7)**. Then you'll use the mark at the top to position the rail before you attach it to the brackets **(Photo 7 inset)**.

Use the stairs as a rail pattern

The next step is to cut the rail and glue on the short horizontal section at the top. Since the rail runs parallel to the stairs, you can use the stair noses as a guide for cutting the rail to the right length and figuring the top angle **(Photos 3–5)**.

Start by cutting a 45-degree angle on one end of the rail. This cut is for the short return to the wall. Rest the cut end on the floor and mark the top **(Photo 3)**. Cut 16-degree angles on the rail and short horizontal sections. This is an approximate angle. You'll test the fit. Trim the cuts until you get a tight fit **(Photos 4 and 5)**. Don't worry if you lose a little length on the rail. It'll just reduce the distance the rail extends at the bottom, which isn't critical. When you're satisfied with the fit, cut the short horizontal rail section to length with a 45-degree miter on the end. Make it long enough to extend a few inches past the next stud so you can add a handrail bracket under it.

The shallow angle makes it difficult to join the short and long rail sections with nails or screws. And dowels or other joining methods require a furniture maker's precision. So instead we'll show you a simple method to join the two with fast-setting epoxy. Cut 2x4s on edge at the same angle as the rail and join them with screws driven at an angle (**Photo 6**). Then support the rail sections with the 2x4s as you press and hold the joint together. With 90-second epoxy, you'll be able to hand-hold the joint together long enough for the epoxy to grab. Concentrate on keeping the profiles exactly lined up and pressing the rails tight together to eliminate gaps. Then leave the joint undisturbed for at least two hours. Overnight would be better, since the epoxy doesn't approach maximum

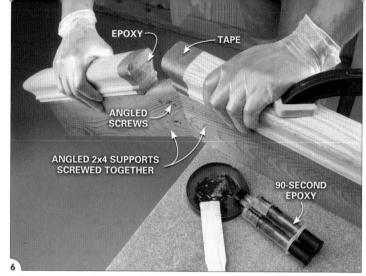

Mix 90-second epoxy for 30 seconds, apply a thin layer to the end of both rail sections, and press and hold the pieces together for one minute until the epoxy starts to set. Carefully remove the protective masking tape after about five minutes. Let the epoxy harden for at least two hours.

Align the top of the handrail with the 36-in. high marks on the tape (see **inset photo**) and mark along the underside of the rail at each stud location.

strength for at least 24 hours. To protect the wood from epoxy that may ooze out, wrap the rail ends with masking tape **(Photo 6)**. Trim excess tape flush to the cut end with a sharp utility knife. Then carefully remove the tape after the epoxy has set for five minutes. The finished joint will probably require sanding to even up the edges. Do this after the epoxy hardens.

Locate and mount the brackets

Photos 7 and 8 show how to mark the underside of the handrail at the stud locations and how to use these marks to align and attach the rail brackets. Position and install two brackets first, one close to the top and one close to the bottom of the rail. **Photo 9** shows how to locate the exact center of the studs. This is an important step because the rail brackets must be centered on the stud or one of the two top screws will miss the framing. Shift the bracket slightly if necessary to center it on the stud. If you shift the bracket, make sure to adjust the height to keep the top aligned with the mark **(Photo 8)**. You may have to patch a few nail holes, but this beats having a bracket pull

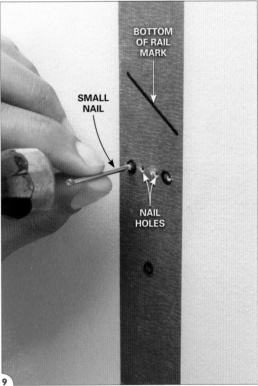

8 Center the rail bracket vertically on the stud and sight across the top to align it with the mark. Then mark all three screw holes. Do this at the studs closest to the top and bottom of the rail.

9 Probe the wall with a finish nail to locate the exact center of the stud. Tap gently to feel when the nail hits solid wood or misses the stud and goes in easily. Shift the bracket if necessary until there's solid wood behind both top holes.

loose. Install the top and bottom brackets first and mount the rail to them **(Photo 12)**. Then add the bracket under the short horizontal section. Finally, sight down the rail and straighten it before adding the intermediate brackets.

Be careful when you drive the screws included with the brackets. The heads will break off easily if you don't predrill pilot holes. If you're driving the screws with a drill, mount the bit in a magnetic bit holder to extend it away from the drill. This will give you more clearance for driving the angled screws.

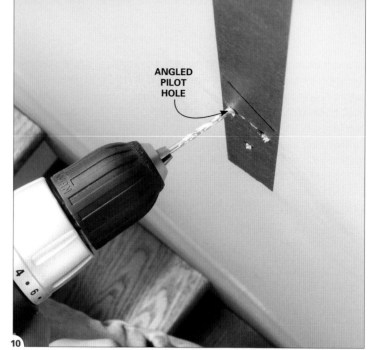

ANGLED PILOT HOLE

10 Drill 1/8-in. pilot holes for the rail bracket screws. You should feel the bit drilling into solid wood. Angle holes slightly toward the center to make sure the screws catch the stud.

RAIL BRACKET

U-SHAPED BRACKET

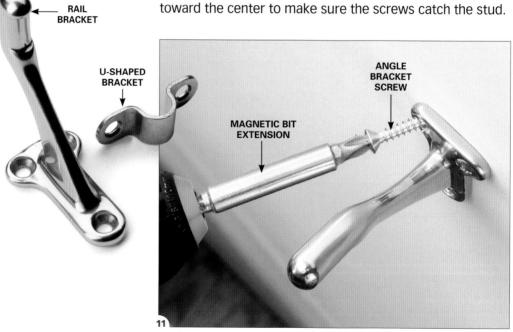

ANGLE BRACKET SCREW

MAGNETIC BIT EXTENSION

11 Remove the masking tape and screw the bracket to the wall. Angle the top screws slightly to follow the angled pilot holes.

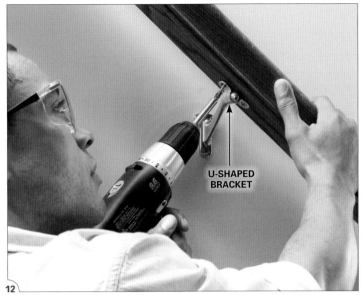

U-SHAPED BRACKET

12

Set the rail on the two brackets and align the top joint with the marks on the tape. Drill pilot holes and then attach the rail to the brackets with the screws and strap provided. Install additional brackets.

Add the returns to complete the rail

With the rail mounted, it's easy to measure for and install the short pieces that return to the wall at the top and bottom of the rail. Measure from the long point of the 45-degree miter on the rail to the wall and add about 1/16 in. for a tight fit. Then cut the returns on your power miter saw. Cut them from longer pieces (at least 12 in.) to avoid getting your fingers too close to the blade. These returns are required by the building code, and for good reason. They eliminate the possibility that loose clothing or a purse strap could get hung up and cause a fall. Besides, they create a nice finished look on the ends of the rail. We attached the returns with wood glue and 4d finish nails, but you could also use the remaining 90-second epoxy. Once the rail is complete, you can take it off to paint or finish it by simply removing the screws from the U-shaped brackets. Since the screw holes are already drilled, it'll be easy to reinstall.

4D FINISH NAILS

WOOD GLUE

MITERED RETURN

13

Cut the short returns on your miter saw. Predrill 1/16-in. holes, then glue and tack the joint with 4d finish nails. Recess the nails with a nail set.

Plant It, Grow It

Plant a tree

If you want your newly planted tree to grow and be healthy, you can't just stick it in a hole in the ground and hope for the best. We'll show you how to plant a tree that will thrive, extend its roots and enhance your landscape. The tree shown is a Summercrisp pear tree, but the steps are the same for any variety.

Pick a tree variety that grows well in your area and soil conditions (a nursery can help you with this). If you're planting a fruit tree, find out if you need to plant a second one within a certain distance for pollination. And ask the nursery (or research online) how big the tree will be when it's full grown. Then plant it far enough away from your house so that once the tree reaches maturity, its branches won't scrape against your siding or roof.

CAUTION

Before you dig a hole for your tree, be sure to call 811 or go to call811.com to have your underground utility lines marked.

1

Take off the plastic. Remove the plastic when you get home, even if you won't plant the tree until the next day. The plastic can suffocate the tree if it's left on too long.

2

Grab a shovel and start digging. Make the hole two to three times as wide as the root ball. As you dig, place the soil on a tarp to make backfilling easier and to avoid damaging surrounding grass.

Plant in the spring or fall

Plant a tree in early spring before the buds open or in the fall before the tree goes dormant. A tree planted during the hot summer months can get stressed and is harder to keep watered. If you insist on a summer planting, keep the soil moist but not sodden. During dry, sunny weather, that might mean watering a few times a day. If you have clay soil and the ground stays damp 3 in. below the surface, you can cut back on watering.

When you buy your tree, ask the nursery to wrap it with plastic for the drive home (our local nursery did it for free). The branches are grouped tightly together so they won't be damaged by wind in the back of a pickup or during unloading. The plastic also keeps the soil from spilling out of the container (although a little water may leak).

Place the tree on its side in the truck bed, strap down the container and wedge scraps of wood under both sides of the container to keep it from rolling around during the drive home. If you're hauling the tree in a van or an SUV, put plastic on the floor to catch any water leaks.

Dig a hole the right size and depth

You want to plant the tree so its root collar—the trunk flare right above the root system— is about 1 in. above ground level. Take the tree out of the container (slitting the container sides) or cut away the wire cage and burlap. Then measure the distance from the root collar to the bottom of the root ball and dig the hole to that depth. Dig the hole two to three times as wide as the root ball.

Don't rely on the container size, the wires or the wrapping around the roots as an indication of the depth you want to plant your tree. If the tree is planted too shallow, the roots could be exposed above the ground, especially as the tree grows. But don't plant it too deep either (a common mistake!). The roots need oxygen to get established, and there's more oxygen near the surface.

Before placing the tree in the hole, break up the tightly wound root ball and carefully fan out the roots. Don't pull too hard or the roots will break. It's OK if some of the soil in the root ball crumbles and falls off. It'll help free the roots. Pulling apart the root ball encourages the roots to expand into the surrounding soil.

You'll have to be careful when you handle the tree, or what's left of the root ball will fall apart and you could tear the smaller roots. Never pick up the tree by its trunk. Instead, support the tree from under or from the side of the root ball. Set the tree in the center of the hole.

Keep the root collar about 1 in. above ground level. If it's too high, remove the tree and dig the hole a little deeper. If the

3

ROOT BALL

Break up the root clump. Gently unwind and spread out the roots so they don't go into the hole as a big ball. But be careful not to break or pull off the thin roots.

4

ROOT COLLAR

Check the root collar height. Lay your shovel across the hole to make sure the root collar is at the right height (ours is too low). If needed, adjust the hole depth.

5

Backfill around the tree. Shovel in the soil evenly around the roots and make sure to keep the tree straight as you fill in around it. The tree will move easily until the hole is completely filled.

trunk flare is too low, add soil under the roots.

Mix the backfill

Don't backfill with only compost manure or peat moss. The roots will be so comfortable in the nutrient-rich backfill that they'll never penetrate the native soil outside the hole.

Mix the backfill material in a wheelbarrow. Use these proportions: two-thirds soil that you dug out of the hole and one-third compost manure. Mix them with a hoe, then use a spade to backfill around the tree. Soak the hole as you backfill. Add backfill until the hole is filled.

Weed trimmers and rodents and other animals can kill a tree by damaging the bark. Install a plastic guard (available at nurseries) over the trunk to protect it. Besides safeguarding against weed trimmer strings and critters, the guard protects young trees against "frost cracking," which happens when the side of the tree that gets more sun grows at a faster rate than the shady side.

Spread a 2- to 3-in.-thick bed of mulch to help the soil hold moisture and to keep weeds from growing. Keep it at least 3 in. from the tree trunk. Mulch, like other organic matter, can have bacteria and fungus, which can spread to the tree and harm or even kill it.

Check your soil before watering

There's no magic formula for how much water to give your tree in its first year. Too little water can kill a tree. But overwatering in clay soil can cause root rot, which can also kill it. The best thing to do is to check your soil conditions. Poke a popsicle stick into the ground near the tree. If the soil is damp down 3 in., you're giving it enough water. If not, water once or twice a day—whatever's needed to keep the soil damp but not saturated.

Run water in the hole. Once the hole is about half filled in, run water around the roots to eliminate air pockets in the soil.

7

Protect the bark. Slip a corrugated tree guard over the trunk. It'll keep weed trimmers, lawn mowers and pesky animals from damaging the bark.

BACKFILL

8

Surround the tree with mulch. Mulch helps maintain moisture in the soil, and it also helps insulate the ground, keeping it cooler in the summer and warmer in the winter.

Grow a great lawn

Water, water, water. Turf specialists make it clear that watering is a key step to a successful lawn. The seeds need to stay moist not only for germination but also for seedling root development. The germinating seeds and the new seedlings are very vulnerable to even short dry periods.

Seed an area that you can realistically keep moist. It may require watering several times a day. An in-ground irrigation system is ideal, but hoses and sprinklers will work. Water long enough to wet the soil to a depth of 3 to 4 in.

Monitor the soil's moistness with the same attention you'd give to a sick child. Be aware of weather conditions; hot sun, high temperatures and wind will dry out the soil quickly. As the soil surface dries, its color will lighten—a sure sign to water again. You won't harm the seeds with too much water unless you're creating runoff and washing the seeds and soil away.

After the seeds have germinated (5 to 20 days), water less often but for longer periods. This deeper watering encourages the seedlings' roots to go deep. After the first mowing, you can begin to cut back on the daily watering.

Three key steps

Loosen the ground to a depth of 4 to 6 in. A rented power tiller will make this job easier. Rake the loosened soil to remove plant material and stones. Break up clumps and finish with a smooth surface.

Apply starter fertilizer and then the grass seed. Sow the seeds in two directions with a drop spreader. Lightly rake the seeds into the soil with a leaf rake. You don't need to bury all the seed, just most of it.

Water to keep the top few inches of soil moist until germination. After germination, apply more water but less often to promote deep roots.

Other key factors

Plant when temperatures are moderate

Avoid planting in the summer when you'll be fighting the hot sun and high temperatures. Also don't plant when the soil is too cold, which prevents germination. A good rule of thumb is to check nearby mature grass. If it's growing (not dormant), then the soil's temperature is OK for seeding. An ideal time to plant is at the end of summer when the soil is quite warm, but cooler days are ahead.

Choose the right seed for your yard and region

Talk to a turf specialist (from a garden center, university extension service or landscaping service) about the right seed for your climate and your specific soil and sun/shade conditions. This is one advantage to growing a lawn from seed. It allows you to fine-tune the type of grass for your yard. Sod, on the other hand, is best suited for those conditions found at the sod farm.

Feed the sprouts

Let's face it: Lawns eat like teenagers, so feeding is a fact of life. Just before seeding, apply a starter fertilizer. Read the product's directions to determine the amount to spread. After the grass has been cut a few times and is established, move to a maintenance feeding schedule consistent with the climate in your region.

5 ways to make your lawn organic

Going organic isn't difficult, but it does take some effort, especially if you're making the switch from chemical fertilizers. And although an organic lawn eventually looks great, it can take two or three years for it to look as thick and deep green each spring as a lawn on a chemical diet. If that sounds OK, then going organic is really about continuing the basic lawn maintenance you've been doing all along, with a few important differences. Here we'll tell you the five most important things you need to do to have a healthy and attractive organic lawn.

Adjust your expectations

You can have a beautiful lawn without chemicals, but it's not going to be as weed-free. Going organic with your lawn means following good basic lawn care practices and using organic fertilizers and natural weed control methods. It also means accepting the reality of a chemical-free lawn—a slower green-up each spring and a lawn with a few more weeds.

Find out what nutrients your soil needs

Testing your soil is crucial, especially if you've been using chemical fertilizers and pesticides, which can destroy soil nutrients and beneficial microbes. Store-bought testing kits aren't very accurate. Instead, contact your local Cooperative Extension Service lab (search for it online). For a small fee, most labs will provide detailed soil collection instructions and pre-addressed soil-testing bags that you can use to send in your soil sample. After testing, the lab will send you specific information about your lawn's soil type, nutrient levels and pH. Most important, the lab will make suggestions for improving your soil.

Because extreme moisture levels and low temperatures can skew pH readings, the best time to test your soil is mid- to late spring or early fall.

Corn gluten can prevent annual weeds, but don't use it when you're overseeding the lawn since it will keep the grass seeds from germinating.

Fight weeds naturally

Over time, a healthy chemical-free lawn will discourage most weeds on its own. But if weeds start to take over, try these options:

- ➤ Pull them manually.
- ➤ Spot-spray with a vinegar or orange oil–based weed killer (available at garden centers).
- ➤ Spread new grass seed over your existing lawn.
- ➤ Sprinkle corn gluten over your lawn in early spring or in fall ($30 for 25 lbs. at garden centers). Corn gluten will prevent crabgrass and other annual weeds, but it takes a few years to become effective.

Top-dress with compost

Add microbes back into your soil by top-dressing your lawn with a 1/2-in. layer of compost once a year. That's about 1 cu. yd. of compost per 1,000 sq. ft. of lawn. Spread it around your yard and use a push broom to sweep it off the grass blades so you don't smother the lawn. Then water it into the soil. This is most effective if you aerate your lawn first.

Compost acts like a sponge to retain moisture and nutrients and adds microbes back into the soil.

Use organic fertilizers

Grass clippings provide about half the nutrients your lawn needs. For the other half, use organic fertilizer, which is made from composted plant waste, manure and other natural materials.

Use your soil test as a guide to selecting the right kind and amount of fertilizer. Organic fertilizers cost about a third more per pound than chemical fertilizers, and you need to use more of them at a time. But since they feed the grass over a longer period of time, you apply them less often and the price difference generally equals out. The main drawback of organic fertilizers is that they release nutrients more slowly, so grass doesn't green up as quickly in the spring.

Feed cool-season grasses before their growth spurt in late May and again in late September to mid-October. Give warm-season grasses frequent light feedings (three to five times) from late spring through early fall.

Wean your lawn from chemicals gradually

If you've had your lawn on a chemical diet and you want to "go green" gradually, here are two things that will help your lawn look better while you make the switch.

> ➤ Use a "bridge" fertilizer that contains both organic and synthetic nitrogen to wean your lawn from chemicals over two to four years. These are typically labeled "organic-based," and the label will list different types of nitrogen. The synthetic nitrogen produces a quicker spring green-up, while the organic nitrogen releases slowly and encourages soil microbes.

> ➤ Reseed your lawn with grass varieties that will work with your existing turf, climate and soil. Talk to your extension service about varieties that require the least fertilizing and watering. Use a mixture of grass species when overseeding to make the lawn less susceptible to drought, disease and weed and insect problems.

Tough plants for paths

THYME

Along with grass, there are quite a number of perennial plants that can be grown between stones in a path. These plants can all tolerate some foot traffic: creeping thyme/mother-of-thyme, woolly thyme, carpet bugleweed/ajuga reptans, creeping jenny/creeping charlie/moneywort, dead nettle/creeping lamium, blue star creeper, brass buttons, mazus reptans and sedum.

To help you select the best ground cover, consider:

➤ The amount of sunlight reaching your path (full sun, partial shade, full shade), because different plants thrive under different conditions.

➤ The amount of traffic the plants will need to endure. Light traffic means the plants will be stepped on once or twice a week. Moderate traffic is once a day. And heavy traffic is similar to walking on your lawn several times a day.

➤ The type of soil (poor or rich) and moisture conditions (wet or dry).

➤ Appearance—plant height, texture and color. If the path is heavily traveled, keep the plant height extremely low to prevent tripping.

Then take your list to a local nursery specialist to walk you through the options best suited for your area. Also note how the plants grow and spread—to determine plant spacing and the number of plants you need to buy. Be sure to avoid plants that are considered invasive species in your area, like creeping jenny (moneywort), which is listed as an invasive species in Tennessee, Wisconsin and the Northeast. You can find this list by visiting plants. usda.gov (click on "Invasive & Noxious"), or ask your local nursery specialist.

Improve the growing conditions when you carve out the soil for your new stone path. It's difficult to grow anything in a trampled area. The soil gets so compacted that roots cannot deliver water and nutrients to the plant. Add good drainage as well as a layer of topsoil at least 1 in. deep around the stones so your ground cover can thrive.

Finally, help your new ground cover prosper with a weekly soaking (the plants need to stay moist) and a weekly hand weeding. And if you'd like to keep the plants short between the stones, consider varieties that tolerate mowing, such as thyme and ajuga.

Here are two sites that offer good, customized information on traffic-tolerant plants for various hardiness zones: jeeperscreepers. info and stepables.com.

Creeping Thyme

(Mother-of-Thyme)
Thymus serpyllum
Zones: 4 through 9 (most of U.S.)
Height: 2 to 4 in.
Plant spreads 12 in.
Full sun to shade
Withstands heavy traffic

Carpet Bugleweed

(Ajuga)
Ajuga reptans
Zones: 3 through 9
Height: 4 to 6 in.
Plant spreads 12 to 18 in.
Full sun to partial shade
Withstands moderate traffic

Creeping Jenny

(Creeping Charlie, Moneywort)
Lysimachia nummularia
Zones: 4 through 8
Height: 2 to 4 in.
Plant spreads 18 to 23 in.
Partial shade
Withstands moderate traffic

Dead Nettle

(Creeping Lamium)
Lamium maculatum
Zones: 4 through 8
Height: 6 to 8 in.
Plant spreads 12 to 23 in.
Partial to full shade
Withstands moderate traffic

It's about thyme

LEMON THYME

CREEPING THYME

Imagine carpeting a sunny area in your yard with a groundcover that is as tough and reliable as grass but requires far less maintenance, covers itself in flowers and smells heavenly. IWe're describing a carpet of thyme. Thyme is a sun-loving herb that likes well-drained soil (not clay). You can even walk on it, so it does well between flagstones in paths and patios.

This delightful herb is hardy to Zone 4 (you can grow it almost everywhere in the United States) and it comes in many different varieties. We like to combine them so that when one variety stops blooming, another begins.

CREEPING THYME

And there are as many different scents as there are flower colors (which, by the way, include white, pink and purple). Leaf colors and growth habits also vary, so you can create a patchwork of contrasting colors, textures and shapes. **Creeping thyme** is a quick grower and tough as nails, with pretty pink flowers. **Woolly thyme** is a ground-hugging plant with fuzzy gray leaves and deep purple flowers. **Lemon thyme** has a lemony fragrance and flavor. **Caraway thyme** tastes like caraway. Check with your local nursery for the varieties that grow best in your region. Space plants 6 in. apart in weed-free, well-tilled soil.

LAMB'S EARS

CREEPING THYME

WOOLLY THYME

Make a hoop greenhouse

Use it to protect seedlings and get an earlier start in the spring. And it'll keep your tender potted plants going longer in the fall.

To make a 4 x 8-ft. hoop house, buy a 10 x 25-ft. sheet of 4-mil plastic and nine 10-ft. lengths of 1/2-in. PVC pipe (inset photo) from a home center. Photos 1–3 show you how to build and use it. Choose a level spot with lots of sunlight and use the dimensions shown in **Photo 1**.

Once you use the third pipe in each group to clamp the plastic in place **(Photo 2)**, your hoop house is ready to use. It dismantles in minutes for winter storage.

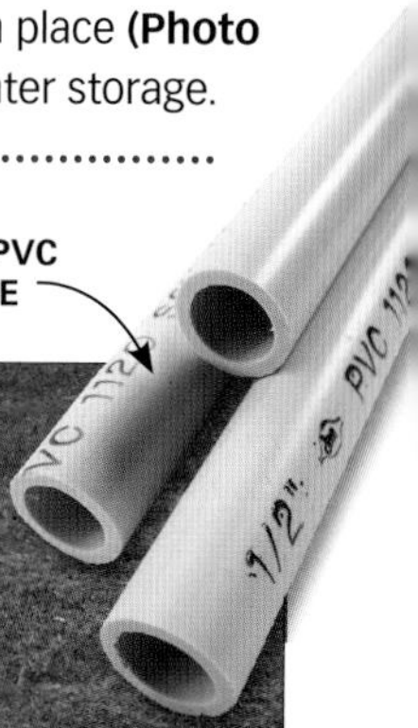

1/2" PVC PIPE

pro tips!

➤ If the ground is hard or gravelly, wedge open the holes by driving a short length of PVC pipe into the ground with a mallet or hammer.

1

Mark the perimeter of your hoop house with twine and stakes. Following our pattern, push one end of each PVC pipe 6 to 8 in. into the ground, bend the pipe gently and push the other end 6 to 8 in. into the ground as well. Place the pipes in pairs spaced about 6 in. apart.

4-MIL
PLASTIC

2

Lay the plastic sheet over the hoops. You can anchor extra material at the ends with heavy rocks. Then push a third pipe into the ground halfway between each pair.

3

Set your seedlings inside the house. Simply slide the plastic up or down for access and to control airflow and heat.

Chapter 6
Store It

One-day garage storage system

This storage system is made mostly from wire shelving and plastic-coated particleboard (called "melamine"). Those two simple materials, along with some clever engineering, provide three big benefits:

- ➤ **Quick, simple construction.** If you can make a few easy cuts (which don't have to be perfect), drive some screws and brush on a little paint, you can build this system in a weekend. If you're an experienced DIYer, you might even be done in a day.

- ➤ **Fits any space.** The system is made up of separate units, so you can build just one, cover an entire wall with several units or leave spaces between units.

- ➤ **Versatile storage.** Aside from wire shelves, the system includes optional hanging spaces for clothes and outdoor gear, plus oversize upper shelves for bulky stuff. As your needs change, you can easily remove or reconfigure the shelves.

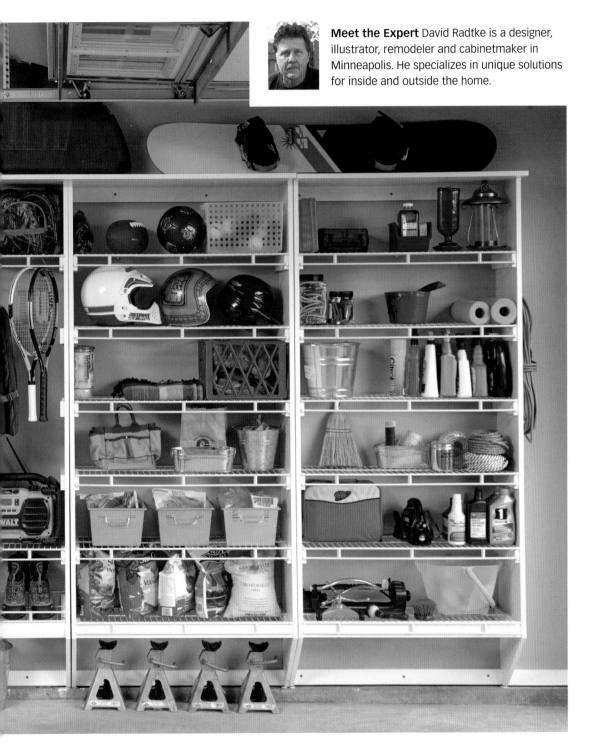

Meet the Expert David Radtke is a designer, illustrator, remodeler and cabinetmaker in Minneapolis. He specializes in unique solutions for inside and outside the home.

Build the units

To get started, cut all the parts (see Cutting List, p. 163). The coating on melamine tends to chip when you cut it. For cleaner cuts, use a 60-tooth carbide circular saw blade and apply painter's tape over the cut (**Photo 1**). Melamine is slippery stuff, so clamp it in place before cutting. Set the depth of your saw blade at 1 in. Chipping won't be a problem when you cut the solid wood parts (B and D). When you cut the supports for the lowest shelves (B1), note that they're shorter than the others. To avoid slow, fussy painting later, paint the wood parts before assembly.

Our shelf spacing is 12 in., but any spacing you choose is fine. Lay pairs of sides (A) next to each other when you mark shelf support locations. That way, you can be sure that the supports will match up after assembly. Drill screw holes (**Photo 2**) and

Cut the sides. Cut one melamine board at a 45-degree angle and use it as a pattern to mark the others for cutting. Mark your cutting line on a strip of painter's tape—the tape reduces chipping as you cut.

Position the shelf supports. Mark where the edge of each shelf support is located and mark a centerline for screw locations. Drill three 9/64-in. screw holes for each support.

then fasten the shelf supports **(Photo 3)**.

Pick out a flat spot on the floor and attach the top (C) to the sides **(Photo 4)**. Then tilt the assembly up a few inches and slide wood scraps beneath it so you can add the rails (D) with 2-in. screws **(Photo 5)**.

SHELF SUPPORT

3

Fasten the shelf supports. Drive 1-1/4-in. screws through the sides and into the shelf supports. A clamp makes this step much easier.

TOP

4

Assemble the unit. Drill holes in the top, then drive cabinet screws to fasten the top to the sides.

With the unit completely assembled, sand the exposed cut edges of the melamine using 150-grit sandpaper, then paint them **(Photo 6)**. Finally, hammer on some furniture glides **(Photo 7)** and the unit is ready for installation.

pro tips!

Choosing screws

We used No. 8 "cabinet" screws throughout this project for three reasons:

➤ The large "washer" heads design looks much neater than a bugle head countersunk into the melamine surface.

➤ The washer heads won't pull through the particleboard.

➤ The coarse threads hold well in particleboard.

Cabinet screws are made by GRK, Spax and other manufacturers.

5

Install the rails. Drill screw holes in the sides and fasten the three rails. You'll need to raise the unit off the floor in order to screw the top and bottom rails.

6

Paint the cut edges. For looks and moisture protection, apply two coats of paint. If you slop a little paint onto the melamine surface, just wipe it off with a damp rag.

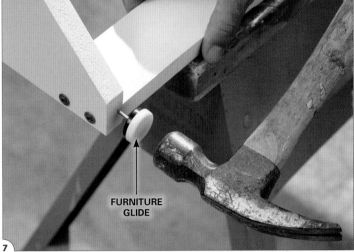

Install the units

If you have finished walls, locate the wall studs with a stud finder and mark them with masking tape. Get some help to lift the assembly up to the wall and hold it in place **(Photo 8)**. Our floor had a row of concrete blocks that protruded from the wall about 1-1/2 in., so we rested the glides on them. The blocks were level but the floor had a slight pitch toward the door, so this saved us the hassle of having to allow for the slope of the floor.

FURNITURE GLIDE

Add glides. Nail plastic furniture glides to the bottom of the sides to keep them from resting directly on damp surfaces, especially concrete.

STUD LOCATION

Install the first unit. Mark the stud locations with painter's tape and set the first unit in place. To ensure that the unit is level and square, check both the top and one side with a level.

9

Add as many units as you like. With the first unit installed square and level, you can simply butt the next unit against it. Screw all units to studs at the top and bottom rungs.

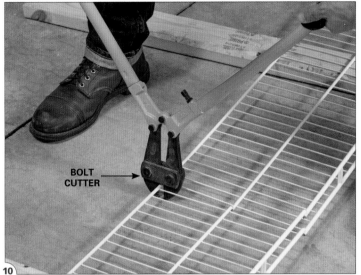

With the assembly against the wall, you can shim underneath to level it (if necessary) and then plumb the sides with a level. Screw it to the wall studs with 2-1/2-in. screws **(Photo 9)**.

If you're willing to spend $35 or so on a bolt cutter, cutting the wire shelves will be quick and easy **(Photo 10)**. Bolt cutters are sized by length; 24 in. is a good choice. When the shelves are cut, set them in place and "clip" them to the wall **(Photo 11)**. Also secure the shelf fronts with coaxial cable staples **(Photo 12)**, which are available in the electrical aisle at home centers.

Cut the shelves. A bolt cutter is the best tool for cutting wire shelving to length. A hacksaw or a metal-cutting blade in a jigsaw will also do the job.

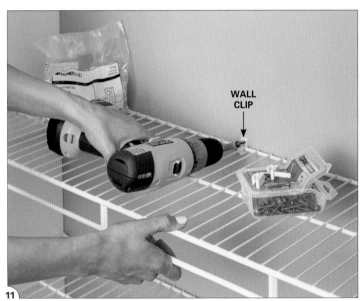

Anchor the shelves. Fasten each shelf to the wall with at least two clips. When you want to fasten the clip to a stud, simply cut off the drywall anchor part of the clip and drive a screw through the clip.

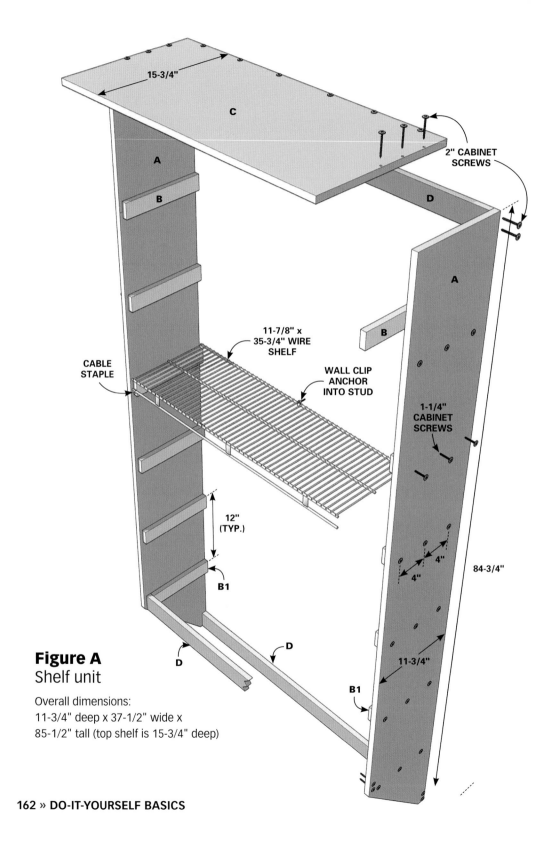

15-3/4"

C

A

B

D

2" CABINET SCREWS

A

B

11-7/8" x 35-3/4" WIRE SHELF

CABLE STAPLE

WALL CLIP ANCHOR INTO STUD

1-1/4" CABINET SCREWS

12" (TYP.)

B1

4"

4"

84-3/4"

D

D

11-3/4"

B1

Figure A
Shelf unit

Overall dimensions:
11-3/4" deep x 37-1/2" wide x
85-1/2" tall (top shelf is 15-3/4" deep)

Cutting List (for one unit)

KEY	QTY.	SIZE & DESCRIPTION
A	2	3/4" x 11-3/4" x 84-3/4" sides (melamine)
B	10	3/4" x 2-1/2" x 11-1/2" shelf supports (pine)
B1	2	3/4" x 2-1/2" x 10-3/4" shelf supports (pine)
C	1	3/4" x 15-3/4" x 37-1/2" top shelf (melamine)
D	3	3/4" x 2-1/2" x 36" rails (pine)

Materials List (for one unit)

ITEM	QTY.
3/4" x 11-3/4" x 8' melamine shelf board	2
3/4" x 15-3/4" x 37-1/2" melamine shelf board	1
3/4" x 2-1/2" x 8' pine boards	3
12" x 12' wire shelving	2
Wire shelving wall clips	12
Wire shelving end caps	12
Coaxial cable staples	12
Cabinet screws (1-1/4", 2", 2-1/2"), 4d (1-1/2") nails	1 pkg. ea.
Furniture glides	2
White paint	1 qt.
150-grit sandpaper	

All of these materials are available at home centers.

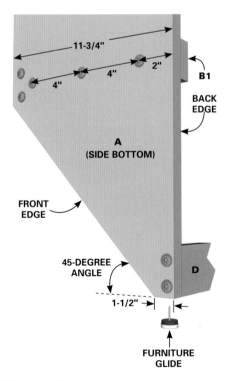

Figure B
Bottom detail

Remove the nails that come with the staples and use 4d nails instead. To store balls or other items that tend to roll off shelves, install a shelf or two upside down. The lip on the front of the shelf keeps stuff in place.

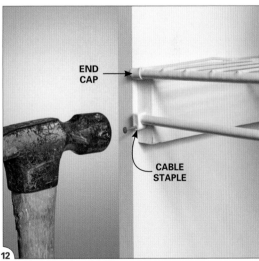

Fasten the shelf fronts. Lock the shelves in place with coaxial cable staples. End caps give the shelves a finished look.

Twin closet shelves

There is a lot of unused real estate above most closet shelves. So, why not add a second shelf above the existing shelf? And the upper shelf could be 15 in. deep instead of 12 in. because there's no closet rod hanging out below. The deep baskets help with the organization; cabinet knobs make for easier access. We show a two-tier shelf; you can install three if your closets (and you) are tall enough.

4-1/2"-TALL BLOCKS

4"-TALL BASKET

Secure blocking to the existing shelf. Buy your baskets, then cut spacer blocks 1/2 in. wider than the baskets are tall. Cut the ends of the blocks at an angle to accommodate the wider top shelf. Screw blocks to the bottom shelf, spacing them 1/2 in. farther apart than the baskets are wide. Then install and secure the top shelf.

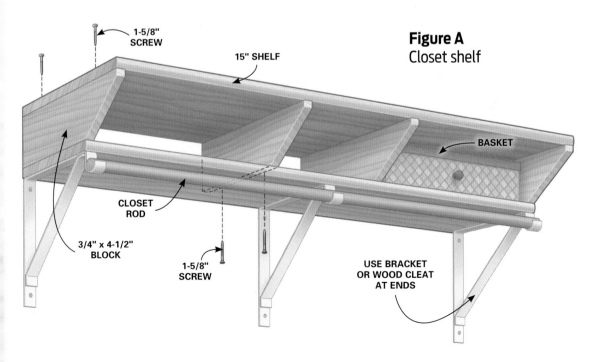

1-5/8" SCREW

15" SHELF

Figure A
Closet shelf

BASKET

CLOSET ROD

3/4" x 4-1/2" BLOCK

1-5/8" SCREW

USE BRACKET OR WOOD CLEAT AT ENDS

PROFESSIONAL
COST: $500

YOUR COST: $150

**SAVINGS:
$350**

COMPLEXITY
Moderate

TOOLS
4-in-1 screwdriver
Air compressor
Air hose
Brad nail gun
Clamps
Cordless drill
Drill bit set
Framing square
Miter saw
Paintbrush
Reciprocating saw
Safety glasses
Self-centering drill bit
Table saw
Tape measure

MATERIALS
1-1/4-in. brad nails
1-5/8-in. screws
1-in. screws
12' of 1x4 pine
3 pairs of drawer
   slides
6' of 1x6 maple
Drawer pulls
One 2' x 4' sheet of
   1/2" birch plywood
One 4' x 8' sheet of
   1/4" birch plywood
Polyurethane
Stain
Wood glue

Under-cabinet drawers

Installing drawers under cabinets sounds like a tough job, requiring fussy planning, the skills of a cabinetmaker and child-size hands to work in that cramped space. But this project is amazingly easy. To simplify the whole process, we designed self-contained drawer units that you can assemble in your shop and then slip into place. To simplify planning, we'll show you three basic measurements that let you size these drawers to fit under any cabinet. Even if you've never built or installed a drawer before, you can do it. This project is economical, too. Our total materials cost for these three drawers was about $150. A cabinetmaker would have charged at least $400 to build and install them. The number of drawers is up to you; install them under all your cabinets or just one.

Will it work with my cabinets?

The vast majority of kitchen cabinets are similar to the ones shown here, with sides that extend to the floor **(see Photo 1)**. But there are a few rare exceptions. Some cabinets, for example, stand on legs rather than the cabinet sides. Open the cabinet doors and take a look at the bottom of the cabinet box. If you see screw heads or holes near the corners, your cabinets probably stand on legs rather than the cabinet sides (the screws or holes allow for height adjustment). In

that case, installing drawers will require different steps than those shown here.

If your cabinets are constructed like these, you can install drawers as shown here. There are just a few things to keep in mind:

➤ If the cabinet is more than 30 in. wide, consider installing two drawers rather than one. Wider drawers tend to bind as you slide them in or out.

➤ Your drawers will be shallow; don't expect to store kettles in them. A

4-in.-high toe space will give you storage space that's about 3 in. deep.

➤ You can install drawers under a sink cabinet (or a bathroom vanity). But if the sink's plumbing runs through the bottom of the cabinet, the drawers will have to be shorter.

Tools and materials

You could build the drawers with nothing but hand tools and a circular saw, but a table saw and miter saw will give you faster, better results. A nail gun

Don't let all this space go to waste. To gain storage space, you usually have to give up space somewhere else. Not in this case. Hidden under almost every kitchen cabinet, there's a cavity containing nothing but air. This low, shallow cavity isn't prime storage space for everyday items, but it's perfect for bakeware, cleaning supplies, pet dishes and more.

is another big time-saver, though you can hammer everything together with 1-1/4-in. finish nails instead.

All the materials are available at most home centers. In the hardware aisle, choose "full-extension" side-mount drawer slides (**see Photo 3**). That way, only 3 to 5 in. of the opened drawer will be covered by the overhanging cabinet front. With cheaper "3/4-extension" slides, only about half the drawer will be accessible. If you can't find full-extension slides, or if you want "overtravel" slides that extend even farther, shop online. Search for "drawer slides" to find online suppliers. Slides are available in 2-in.-length increments. Most cabinets accept 18- or 20-in. slides.

Choose hardwood plywood like birch or oak for your drawers. Construction-grade tends to warp. Most home centers carry plywood in 2 x 4-ft. and/or 4 x 4-ft. sheets, so you don't have to buy a full 4 x 8 sheet. Pick out straight pine 1x4s for the cradle sides. For the drawer faces, you'll need hardwood that matches your cabinets. If your toe-space height is 4 in. or less, a 1x4 board will do. For a taller toe space, you'll need a 1x6. Most home centers carry only a few types of wood such as oak, cherry, and birch or maple. If your cabinets are made from a less common species, look for a lumberyard that carries a wider

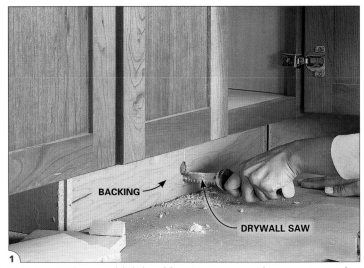

1 Break out the toe-kick backing to open up the spaces under the cabinets. Just drill a hole near the center, cut the backing in half and pull it out.

2 Build super-simple drawer boxes. Just glue and nail the sides, front and back together, then glue and nail on the plywood bottom.

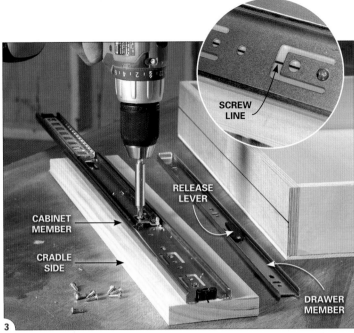

SCREW LINE

CABINET MEMBER

CRADLE SIDE

RELEASE LEVER

DRAWER MEMBER

3 Mount the slides, centering the screw holes on the screw lines. Press the release lever to separate the drawer member from the cabinet member.

selection. Or improvise—with the right stain, you can make birch or maple approximately match the color of just about any wood. The grain may look different, but that difference usually isn't noticeable in the dark toe space. The drawers shown here have maple faces, even though the cabinets are made from cherry.

Remove the toe-kick and measure

Before you buy materials, open up the cavity under the cabinets so you can take measurements. First, pull off the "toe-kick," the strip of plywood or particleboard in the toe space. Usually, the toe-kick is held by just a few small

Figure A
Drawer unit
The drawer, cradle and slides form a complete unit that's simple to build and easy to install under a cabinet.

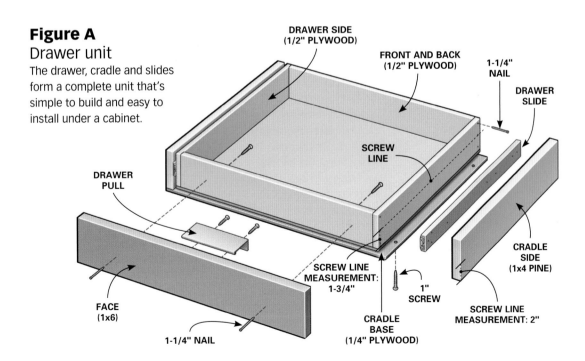

DRAWER SIDE (1/2" PLYWOOD)

FRONT AND BACK (1/2" PLYWOOD)

1-1/4" NAIL

DRAWER SLIDE

SCREW LINE

DRAWER PULL

SCREW LINE MEASUREMENT: 1-3/4"

1" SCREW

CRADLE SIDE (1x4 PINE)

FACE (1x6)

1-1/4" NAIL

CRADLE BASE (1/4" PLYWOOD)

SCREW LINE MEASUREMENT: 2"

Figure B
Drawer sizing simplified

MEASUREMENT "A"

➤ Subtract 1-1/2 in. from "A" to determine the width of drawer sides, front and back.

➤ Subtract 1/2 in. from "A" to determine the width of drawer faces. The length of each face depends on the width of the cabinet.

MEASUREMENT "B"

➤ Subtract 3-3/4 in. from "B" to determine the length of the drawer front and back. This will make the entire drawer/cradle assembly 1/4 in. smaller than the width of the cavity.

MEASUREMENT "C"

➤ Subtract 1/4 in. from "C" to determine the length of the cradle and drawer sides.

➤ This is also the maximum length of the drawer slides you can use.

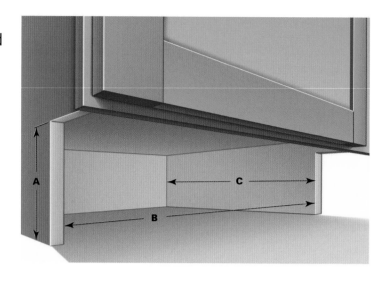

nails and is easy to pry off. If you don't plan to cover the entire toe space with drawers, be gentle so you can later cut the toe-kick to length and reinstall a section. If layers of flooring have been added since the cabinets were installed, you'll have to pull the top edge of the toe-kick outward first and then pry it up to clear the built-up floor.

Next, remove the toe-kick backing under the cabinets (**Photo 1**). Simply drill a 1-in. hole and cut the backing with a drywall saw. Then grab a flashlight and check for obstructions. Break out any blocking with a chisel or pry bar. Pull out or cut off any nails. Now you're ready to take the three measurements to determine the sizes of the drawers. There's no need for complex calculations—it's all reduced to simple subtraction in **Figure B**.

Build drawers and cradles

If you've ever installed drawer slides similar to the ones shown here, you already know how fussy they are. They require a precise 1/2-in. space on both sides of the drawer—build a drawer that's a hair too wide or narrow and you've got a drawer that won't budge. To sidestep that precision work, build each drawer first and then build a "cradle" around it. If you want to install two drawers under one wide cabinet, build a single cradle with both drawers sharing one of the cradle sides and the cradle base.

These drawers are as easy as they get: Just nail them together (**Photo 2**). If you're using finish nails rather than a nail gun, predrill so you don't split the plywood parts. Remember to place the front and back

CRADLE BASE

CRADLE SIDE

4

Add the cradle base to create a self-contained drawer unit. Fasten the base with screws only; glue could drip down and gum up the slides.

between the sides. Then measure and cut the drawer bottoms. As you install each bottom, be sure the drawer box is square using a large carpenter's square or by using the plywood bottom as a guide (this only works if you've cut the bottoms perfectly square). Cut the 1x4 cradle sides to the same length as the drawer sides. In most cases, you can use 1x4s at full width (3-1/2 in.). But if your toe-space height (measurement "A" in **Figure B**) is less than 4 in., cut the cradle sides to a width 1/2 in. less than the toe-space height.

Next, mark screw lines on the drawer and cradle sides (**see Figure A** for measurements). Pull each slide apart to separate the drawer member from the cabinet member. Then screw them on (**Photo 3**). Our drawer and cradle sides were the same length as the drawer slides—yours may not be. So be sure to position the front ends of each drawer member and cabinet member flush with the fronts of the drawer and cradle sides. Slip the slides back together, lay the drawer upside down and screw on the cradle base (**Photo 4**). Then flip the whole unit over and inspect your work. Make sure the drawer opens smoothly. When the drawer is closed, the front of it should be flush with the cradle sides, give or take 1/16 in. Any problems are easy to fix by removing screws

and repositioning the slides. **Note:** With these drawer units assembled, the cradle sides are exactly the same height as the drawers. Your drawers may come out a bit higher or lower.

Install the drawers

Before you remove the drawers from their cradles, number them to avoid mix-ups later. Each drawer will slide smoothest in the cradle that was built for it. Slip each cradle into place and fasten it to the cabinet with four 1-5/8-in. screws. If you have flooring that's more than 1/4 in. thick, first set scraps of 1/4- or 1/2-in. plywood under the cabinet to support the cradle. The cradle base can be higher

CRADLE

5

Slip the cradle under the cabinet and drive screws through the cradle sides
just below the slides. Small hands and a small drill make this part easier.

than or flush with the flooring, but not lower than the flooring. Position the cradle sides flush with the cabinet sides and tight against one side **(Photo 5)**. Screw the cradle to the cabinet, starting with the tight side. On the other side, don't drive in the screws so hard that you distort the cradle. If the drawer doesn't glide smoothly, slightly loosen those screws. Also be sure the drawer doesn't drag on the floor when opened. Load a few heavy objects into the drawer and open it. If it drags, remove the front screws from the cradle and slip washers under it. That will give the drawer a slight upward tilt to clear the floor.

Next, cut the drawer faces to width. When you cut them to length, avoid measuring mistakes by marking them while they're in place. Leave a 1/8- to 1/4-in. gap between neighboring faces. At the end of a row of cabinets, make the face flush with the outer side of the cabinet. The method shown to attach the faces works best with a nail gun **(Photo 6)**. Driving nails with a hammer can knock the drawer or cradle out of position. If you don't have a nail gun, stick the faces in place with double-face carpet tape. Then pull out each drawer and attach the face by driving two 1-in. screws from inside the drawer. With the faces

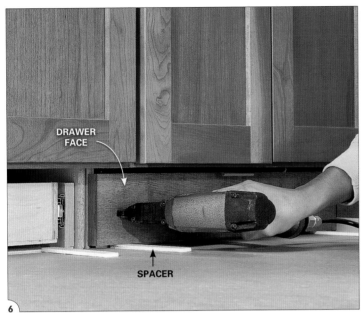

DRAWER FACE

SPACER

6

Rest the drawer faces on 1/4-in. spacers. Tack the face in place with two nails, then open the drawer and drive screws into the face from the inside of the drawer box.

attached, be sure they don't drag on the floor. If necessary, raise them with washers.

Finishing up

Remove the drawers from their cradles for finishing. Unscrew the slides from the drawers and sand the drawer faces with 120-grit sandpaper. Also prepare a few stain-testing blocks, using leftover scraps from the faces and sanding them. You can remove one cabinet door and take it to a paint store to have matching stain custom-mixed. If you have the patience to experiment, you could buy a couple of cans of stain and mix them to create your own.

Either way, apply the stain to your test blocks before you stain the faces. The match doesn't have to be perfect, since the faces will be shaded by the overhanging cabinet fronts. After staining the faces, finish the drawers—faces and boxes—with two coats of water-based polyurethane. Before reinstalling the drawers, add the drawer pulls or knobs. If you can't find pulls that closely match your existing cabinet hardware, you could choose pulls like these that fit over the tops of the drawer faces and are hidden under the cabinets. To find similar pulls online, search for "EPCO architectural pull."

Materials List

Here's what was used to build drawers to fit under three 24-in.-wide cabinets. Your quantities may differ.

One 4' x 8' sheet of 1/4" birch plywood

One 2' x 4' sheet of 1/2" birch plywood

12' of 1x4 pine

6' of 1x6 maple

3 pairs of drawer slides

Drawer pulls, wood glue, stain, polyurethane, 1-1/4" brads or nails, 1" and 1-5/8" screws.

Hidden bathroom storage cabinet

Got plans to hang a mirror or a large painting? Consider using the stud cavity behind it for handy, secret storage. I installed this mirror cabinet in the bathroom—like a giant medicine cabinet. The mirror glides on ball-bearing drawer slides to open and close the cabinet. When the mirror is in place, nobody knows the cabinet is even there!

Meet the Expert
Brad Holden, a senior editor, has been building cabinets and furniture for more than 30 years.

Getting started

Including the frame, my mirror was 21-1/4 in. wide, so I needed about 23 in. of open wall space to the left of the mirror for it to slide left. You can mount the drawer slides to go either direction.

I bought a frameless beveled mirror for $125. I could have purchased a framed mirror to save some work, but I decided to build my own frame. The mirror is heavy, so I wanted the frame to be solid lumber for strength. I also needed it to be thick enough for 3/4-in. screws to attach the drawer slides.

I chose 1x4 poplar boards. Poplar is easy to find, inexpensive and lightweight. It also has good screw-holding capability and takes paint well. For the cabinet, I used precut melamine shelving from the home center. Its front edge is already banded, so if you plan your cuts, you won't need to edge-band your shelves.

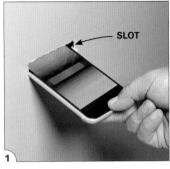

1

2

1. **Peek inside the wall.** Check for obstructions in the wall cavity. Cut a slot big enough for your phone and take one photo up and one down. If there are pipes or electrical cables in your way, you can choose a different stud cavity, size the cabinet so it doesn't interfere or reroute the pipes or wires. If you pick a different location, you can easily patch the small slot.

2. **Cut the opening.** Starting from the slot, cut a hole large enough to reveal the exact stud locations. Draw the opening using a level and a framing square, and then cut on the line.

Figure A
Stud-space storage

Overall Dimensions:
65-1/4" H x 21-1/4" W x 5-1/4" D

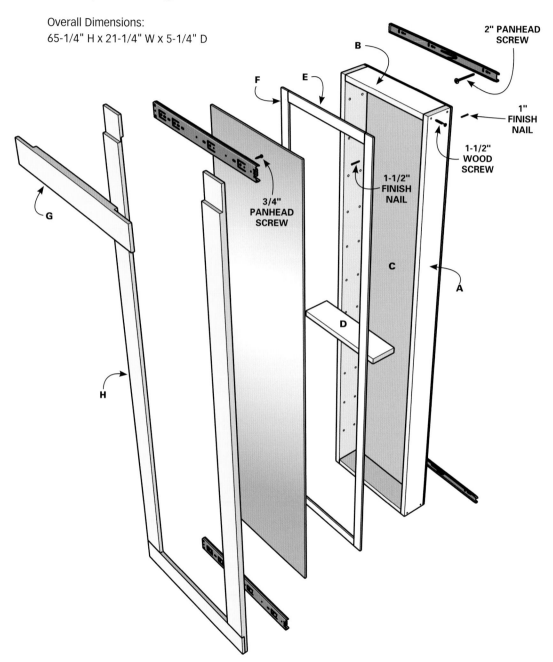

2" PANHEAD
SCREW

1"
FINISH
NAIL

1-1/2"
WOOD
SCREW

1-1/2"
FINISH
NAIL

3/4"
PANHEAD
SCREW

A
B
C
D
E
F
G
H

Figure B
Half-lap joint

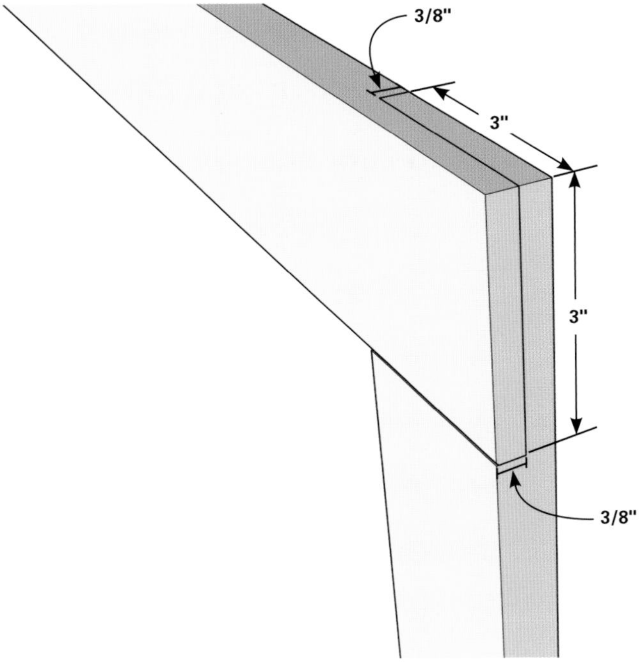

3/8"

3"

3"

3/8"

Figure C
Rabbet

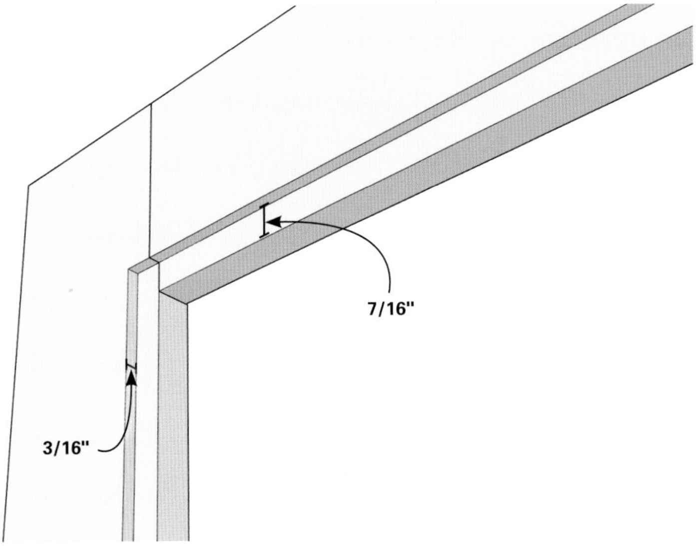

7/16"

3/16"

Figure D
Cutting diagram

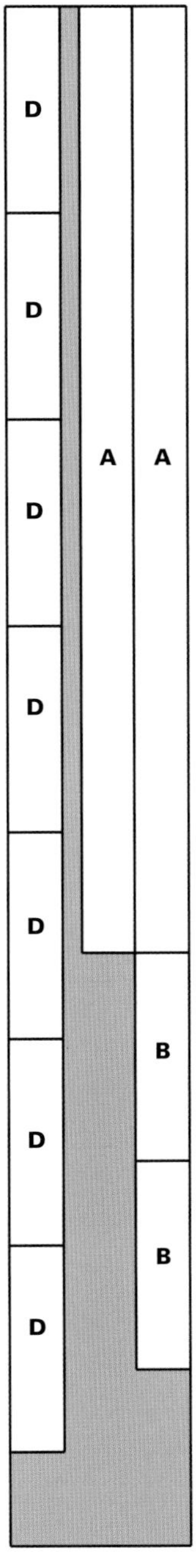

D

D

D

A A

D

D

B

D

B

D

3. Build the shelves. Cut a strip for the shelves (D) from the front edge of the melamine. Next, cut the sides (A), top and bottom (B) from the remaining piece **(see Figure D)**. Assemble the parts using 1-1/2-in. wood screws. Cut the back (C) and paint it white. You may need to resize the cabinet slightly to fit your stud cavity.

4. Drill for shelf supports. Make a jig to drill the holes by drilling evenly spaced holes in a length of hardwood. Hold the jig in place on the cabinet side and drill the first hole. Slip a drill bit of the same size into the hole you just drilled to keep the jig in place. When you get to the end of the jig, slip the drill bit into the last hole and continue. Use a depth stop on the bit to ensure you won't drill through the side. Nail on the back with 1-in. finish nails.

3

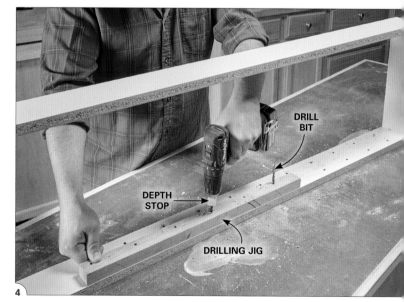

DRILL BIT

DEPTH STOP

DRILLING JIG

4

5. **Add the trim.** Glue and nail on the trim (E and F) to cover the edges of the cabinet as well as any gap between the cabinet and the wall opening. Choose trim that's 3/8 in. thick or less. Because standard drawer slides are 1/2 in. thick and the wall may not be dead flat, thicker trim could keep the mirror from sliding.

6. **Cut half-lap joints.** Cut the frame parts (G and H) to length, then make half-lap joints at their ends. I cut half-laps using a dado set on my table saw. I attach a long fence to the miter gauge, and then add a stop block to set the joint's shoulder. Start with two scrap pieces, making passes in both until you get the right depth.

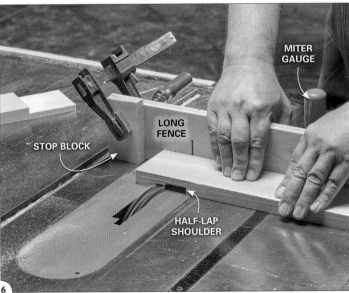

MITER GAUGE

LONG FENCE

STOP BLOCK

HALF-LAP SHOULDER

7. Chamfer the joints.
Add a very slight chamfer to the shoulders of the joints on the side pieces and on the entire inner edge of the top and bottom. This creates a shallow "V" where the joints come together. The groove is optional but adds some visual interest. I like to use a block plane for this, but a sanding block works fine.

8. Assemble the frame.
Glue the half-lap joints, and then clamp them until the glue dries. Set the frame on blocks or sawhorses to provide room for the clamp heads. Because of their ample gluing surface, these half-lap joints are super-strong.

CHAMFER

7

8

MIRROR RECESS →

9

9. Rout the mirror recess.

Rout a 7/16-in.-wide recess the depth of your mirror's thickness, using a rabbeting bit in your router. To avoid router tear-out, make the cut in two or three passes. Sand the mirror frame up to 150 grit and then apply paint.

10. Attach the slides.

Separate the two components of the drawer slides. Fasten the wide tracks to the frame. If you mount the narrow tracks to the frame, the slides' release levers won't be accessible. Placement of the slides isn't critical; just center them side to side and be sure they're above and below the cabinet's trim.

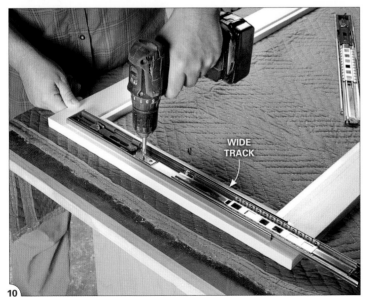

WIDE TRACK

10

11. **Install blocking.** The drawer slides don't carry weight the usual way, so they must be firmly attached to the wall. Instead of relying on drywall anchors, I installed blocking. Using the drawer slide placement on the frame to determine where the slides would attach to the wall, I cut 2x4s to fit between the studs and screwed them into place. Mark centerlines on the wall for the drawer slide locations.

12. **Install the cabinet.** Set the cabinet in the opening, plumb and level. Fasten it into place with 3-in. wood screws through the sides, into the studs.

12

11

13. Hang the frame. Fasten the top narrow track on its centerline above the cabinet, centered side to side. Slip the other narrow track into its wide track at the bottom of the frame, making sure the narrow track is fully extended. Slide the frame onto the top narrow track. Plumb the frame, and then fasten the bottom narrow track to the wall.

TOP NARROW TRACK

BOTTOM NARROW TRACK

13

14. Apply safety backer.
This mirror will be in motion regularly, so I applied transparent window safety film on the back. In case of breakage, the glass shards won't crash to the floor. Just peel the backing and press the film onto the back of the mirror. Since this isn't a window, I wasn't picky about removing every last air bubble.

15. Install the mirror.
It's easier to hang the frame by itself, without the added weight, so I installed the mirror last. Apply a bead of silicone in the rabbet, and then carefully place the mirror in the silicone. Let the silicone set for a day and then trim off any excess with a razor blade before hanging the mirror.

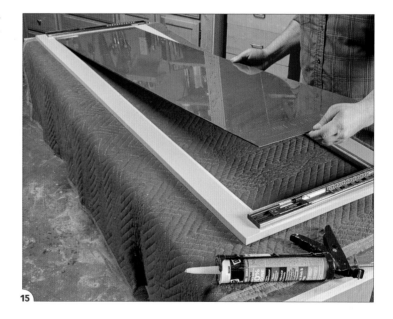

Materials List

ITEM	QTY.
16" x 60" mirror	1
3/4" x 12" x 96" melamine shelf	1
1/4" x 48" x 96" plywood	1
1/4" x 1-1/2" mullion	15'
1x4 x 8' poplar boards	2
18" full-extension drawer slides (screws included)	2
Shelf supports	28
No. 6 x 2" panhead screws	8
No. 8 x 1-1/2" wood screws	8
1" finish nails	
3/4" panhead screws	8
Clear silicone	
Paint	1 qt.
Wood glue	
Glass safety film	

Cutting List

KEY	QTY.	DIMENSIONS	PART
A	2	3/4" x 3-3/4" x 59"	Cabinet sides
B	2	3/4" x 3-3/4" x 13"	Cabinet top and bottom
C	1	1/4" x 14-1/2" x 59"	Cabinet back
D	7	3/4" x 3-3/4" x 12-7/8"	Shelves
E	2	1/4" x 1-1/4" x 13"	Trim rails
F	2	1/4" x 1-1/4" x 60"	Trim stiles
G	2	3/4" x 3" x 21-1/4"	Frame rails
H	2	3/4" x 3" x 65-1/4"	Frame stiles

Painting gear hangout

Organize your paint brushes, scrapers, roller frames, rags and paint cans with this shelf made from two 1x8 boards screwed together and reinforced with metal shelf brackets We built this one 38 in. long to fit three brackets of sliding spring grips that we mounted under the shelf for tool storage. Build and attach this shelf to a shop or basement wall, and you'll thank reader Steve Sampson for enforcing orderly storage on all your far-flung painting paraphernalia.

DRIVE SCREWS THROUGH SHELF BOARD INTO LOWER BOARD'S EDGE

TWO 1x8 BOARDS

SHELF BRACKET

SPRING CLAMP BRACKET

Yard tool slant rack

Stashing stuff in the unused spaces between studs is a smart move; adding these slant boxes to expand the space is smarter yet. They give your tools more "headroom" and give you easier access to long- and short-handled tools.

For the tall unit, use the bottom wall plate for the bottom of your box. Attach the plywood to create a 1-in. gap at the bottom for removing dirt or dropped items. For the shorter slant boxes, install your own blocking to create the bottom; leave a gap at the bottom of the plywood for those, too. We show 48-in. and 16-in. versions; you can make yours any depth or length you want. **Note:** If your garage has a short ceiling (or your tools have extra-long handles), create a cutout in the top of the plywood face, as shown in **Figure A**, to allow more entrance and exit leeway for your tools.

Rip a 2x4 diagonally to create the sides. Screw each wedge to the face of a stud. Install a plywood face and you're ready to store stuff.

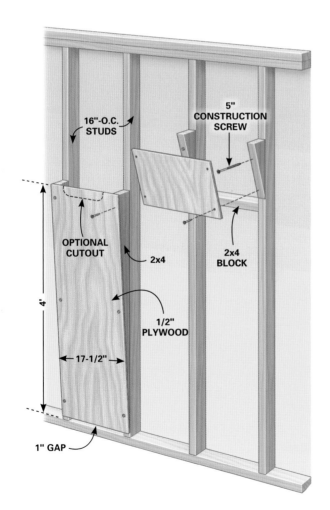

Figure A
Slant rack

16"-O.C. STUDS

5" CONSTRUCTION SCREW

OPTIONAL CUTOUT

2x4

2x4 BLOCK

1/2" PLYWOOD

4'

17-1/2"

1" GAP

Stand-up tool caddy

When you need to carry your tools to the task at hand, you could use a toolbox. But unlike a toolbox, this slick tool caddy puts all your necessary tools in plain sight. With a little imagination, it can be configured to hold whatever tools or fasteners you like. The caddy stands up on its own when in use and hangs flat on the wall between projects.

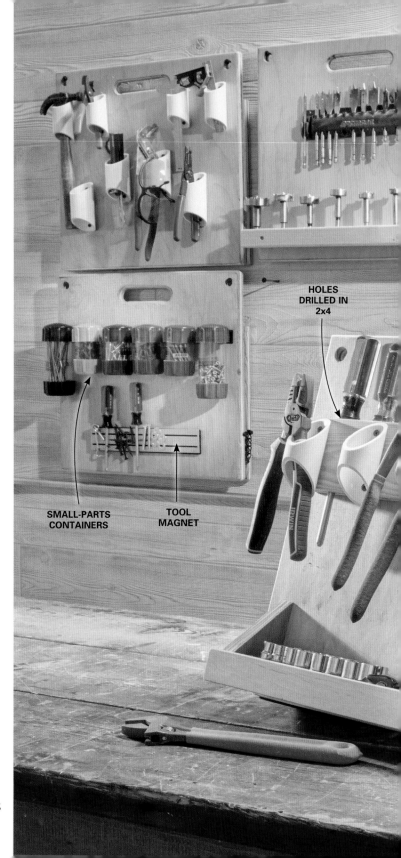

HOLES DRILLED IN 2x4

SMALL-PARTS CONTAINERS

TOOL MAGNET

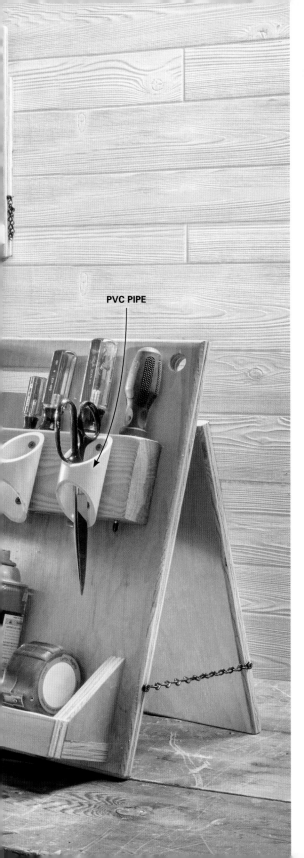

PVC PIPE

- ➤ A generous handle makes carrying easy. Drill a starter hole and then cut out the rest with a jigsaw.
- ➤ You can make them any size you'd like, but 18 x 18 in. holds lots of stuff and is a nice carrying size.
- ➤ Hanger holes are centered 16 in. apart, so you can hang the caddies on lag screws driven into studs.
- ➤ You can install whatever tool-holding system suits your needs.
- ➤ Cut PVC at an angle so you have space to drive the mounting screws.
- ➤ Two-inch butt hinges connect the prop to the tool panel.
- ➤ The chain stabilizes the open caddy.

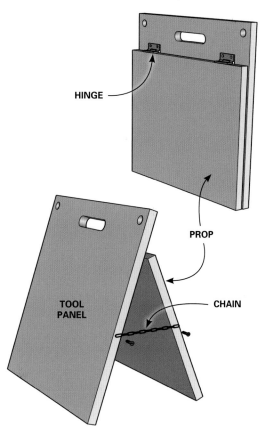

HINGE

PROP

TOOL PANEL

CHAIN

Chapter 7
Play It Safe

Sweep the roof as you work to remove debris and loose shingle granules that cause slippery footing. Keep the lanyard adjusted to minimize slack in the rope between you and the roof anchor. Tie or wire the top of the extension ladder to nails set in the rafter ends.

PERSONAL FALL ARREST SYSTEM

SHOES THAT GRIP

ROOF FREE OF DEBRIS AND LOOSE GRANULES

SLIDE GUARD (ROOF BRACKETS WITH 2x6)

Roof safety

Let's face it—roofs are dangerous places. But sooner or later you'll have to clamber up there to fix a leak, replace a vent or evict a family of squirrels. Here we'll show you a few simple ways to make roof work a lot safer.

A minimal investment in roof brackets will immediately reward you with much greater roof safety and convenience. But if you have to spend a lot of time up there or have an especially steep roof, we recommend that you also buy a roof harness system. It's the next best thing to a parachute. We'll tell you what to buy and how to use it, and give you some general roofing safety tips too.

Getting up to the roof safely is the first step

If you don't own one already, buy or rent a sturdy extension ladder that extends at least 3 ft. above the roof edge. Aluminum is the lightest, but fiberglass ladders provide better protection against electrocution in case the ladder accidentally touches a power line or live wire. If possible, set the ladder on firm, level ground. On uneven ground, place squares of plywood under one foot to level the ladder base, and then secure it with wire or rope tied to stakes. Fasten the top of the ladder with rope or wire tied to a secure anchoring point such as a 20d nail driven into a rafter. That will keep it from sliding sideways as you step onto the roof **(opening photo)**.

Stepping from the ladder to the roof or from the roof to the ladder is precarious and can be unnerving. Here are a few pointers to make it easier and safer:

➤ If possible, avoid carrying anything up the ladder. Use a helper and a bucket tied to a rope to hoist up tools and supplies.

➤ Extend the top of the ladder at least 3 ft. above the roof edge so you'll have something to hang on to as you step onto and off the roof. Never step on any of the ladder rungs above the roof.

➤ Keep two hands on the top rung of the ladder as you step onto and off the roof.

LADDER
TIED AT TOP

Build a 'slide guard' with roof brackets and 2x6s as a first line of defense

Once you're safely up to the roof, you'll want to set up roof brackets and planks all along the eave **(opening photo)**. These serve a dual purpose. They allow you a safe place to step onto and rest tools and materials. And they also act as a slide guard that will help prevent you from falling off the edge of the roof if you lose your footing higher up and slide down.

Photos 1 and 2 show how to fasten the brackets to the roof and secure the planks. Each roof bracket should have a label on it with complete instructions. Read and follow them carefully.

pro tips!

Roof smarts

When it comes to roofs, even the best safety equipment is no substitute for common sense and good judgment. Here are some tips for working safely on a roof:

➤ Leave steep and/or high roof work to the pros. The few dollars you'll save by doing it yourself aren't worth the risk of death or a lifelong disability if you fall.

➤ Pick a clear, calm, cool time of day to work on roofs. Wet roofs are slippery. Wind also poses a danger, and excessive heat softens the shingles, making them vulnerable to damage.

➤ Wear shoes with a soft rubber sole for extra traction.

➤ Keep the bottom of your shoes free of mud and dirt, and the roof swept clear of dirt and debris.

➤ Rope or mark off the ground beneath your work area to let people below know you're working above. Even the most careful worker eventually drops a tool off the roof. Always look and call out before tossing anything down.

➤ When you're not using your power tools, secure them with short lengths of rope or bungee cords. Keep hand tools and supplies in a 5-gallon bucket hung on a roof bracket. Carefully position ropes and extension cords so they're not underfoot; they're very slippery.

➤ Stay off slate and tile roofs. Loose tiles or slate can fall out and the surfaces are easily damaged if you're not experienced.

SHINGLE TAB

20D NAIL INTO RAFTER

90-DEGREE ROOF BRACKET

1

1. **Nail** a row of roof brackets about 18 in. up from the eave and about 4 ft. apart. Position the brackets directly over a rafter or truss **(Fig. A)**. Install each bracket by lifting a shingle tab and sliding the bracket under it. Then pound 20d common nails into each slot, making sure they hit the rafter or truss.

Figure A
Roof bracket nailing

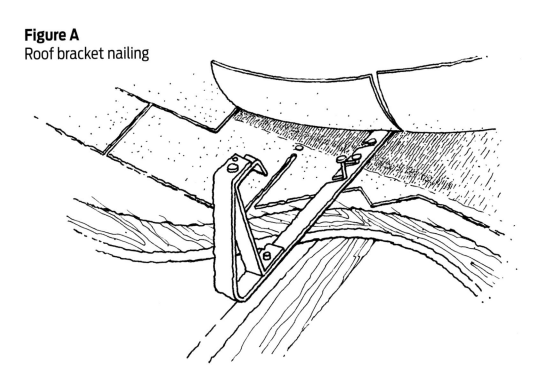

First locate a truss or rafter—the roof brackets must be nailed through the sheathing and into these structural members. The exposed rafter tails on our roof made this easy. If you're not so lucky, listen and feel for a solid spot as you tap across the roof with a hammer. When you locate solid wood, carefully slide the blade of a pry bar under the shingle to separate it from the shingle underneath, and gently bend the tab up. Then you can place the nails where they'll be covered by the shingle (**Photo 1**). If you feel the nail miss the rafter (it will penetrate easily), pull it out and put a dab of caulk or plastic roofing cement on the hole to seal it. Then move the nail over an inch and try again.

Rafters in older homes are usually 16 in. apart, while trusses in newer homes are usually 24 in. apart. Both have 1-1/2 in. of nailing surface. Measure from the first bracket to find more rafters or trusses. Complete the slide guard by adding the 2x6 plank (**Photo 2**). Now you can safely work your way up the roof by adding more brackets and planks about every 8 ft.

2. **Lay** a 2x6 plank across the brackets and attach it to the brackets with screws. Make sure the 2x6 extends at least 6 in. but not more than 12 in. past the end brackets. Set another row of roof brackets and planks about every 8 ft. up the roof, or as close together as needed to make your work safe and convenient.

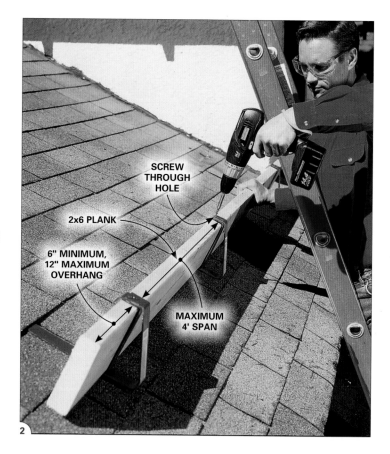

SCREW THROUGH HOLE

2x6 PLANK

6" MINIMUM, 12" MAXIMUM OVERHANG

MAXIMUM 4' SPAN

2

3. **Strap** on the safety harness according to the manufacturer's instructions. Tighten the straps for a snug fit. Double-check all the buckles before you go onto the roof.

SAFETY HARNESS

ADJUSTABLE CHEST STRAP

PARACHUTE BUCKLE

PASS BUCKLE

PASS BUCKLE

Buying roof safety gear

Safety harness

The harness is only one part of a personal fall arrest system. It's called a "system" because all the components—the harness, lanyard, rope-grab, rope and roof anchor—are carefully engineered to work together. One brand is DBI/SALA (globalindustrial.com/c/safety/protection). The company sells "roofer anchor kits" with everything you'll need. Consider splitting the cost with friends or neighbors and sharing the kit.

Most carpenters and roofers have had a close call on a roof, but most will readily admit they were doing something stupid at the time. Roofs are inherently dangerous places, but if you follow our suggestions and stay focused on safety, you'll greatly reduce the chances of an accident. And with the roof brackets and personal fall arrest system in place, if you do slip, at least you'll live to tell about it.

Roof brackets

Roof brackets are available at hardware stores, lumberyards, roofing suppliers and home centers. Buy enough 90-degree brackets **(Photo 1)** to place one bracket every 4 ft. along the edge of the roof below where you'll be working. Use brackets designed to hold a 2x6. Larger planks are too hard to step over when you're getting onto the roof. You'll want additional rows of brackets and planks about 8 ft. apart across the roof to rest supplies on and provide secure footing.

Buy the best 2x6s you can find. Make sure the knots are small (under 1 in. diameter) and don't go all the way through the board.

When you're done on the roof, remove the brackets and planks in the opposite order, starting at the top and working down **(Photo 6)**.

You can't just tie a rope to your belt

On low-pitched roofs where footing is no problem and the eaves are less than 12 ft. or so from the ground, you may feel safe working with just roof brackets and planks in place. This is OK. But for the ultimate in roof safety, especially on steeper roofs or big jobs, invest in a safety harness and rope. (See "Buying roof safety gear" on p. 199.)

Photos 4 and 5 show how to set up the harness and rope (technically called a "personal fall arrest system"). The roof anchor must be fastened securely to solid wood like a rafter, truss or ridge beam, not just through the roof boards or plywood. Models vary

4. Fasten the roof anchor to the peak according to the manufacturer's instructions. We drove six 1/4 x 2-in. lag screws through the roof boards into the rafters. Predrill 3/16-in. holes. Then use a wrench to tighten the lag screws.

SOCKET WRENCH

ROOF ANCHOR

1/4" x 2" LAG SCREWS

4

slightly, so read the manufacturer's instructions and follow them carefully. Here are a few of the key points:

➤ Inspect the harness and lanyard for loose stitching and worn webbing. Never reuse a harness or lanyard that has been subjected to a fall. Send them back to the manufacturer for inspection. Examine the rope for fraying.

➤ Adjust the harness buckles for a snug fit.

➤ Locate the roof anchor directly above where you'll be working on the roof. Don't work more than 4 ft. to the side of the roof anchor. Relocate the anchor or add more anchors if necessary.

➤ Mount the roof anchor to the peak no closer than 6 ft. from the edge of the roof.

➤ Reposition the rope-grab as you work to minimize the amount of slack in the rope between you and the roof anchor.

5

6

5. **Clip** the end of the safety rope to the ring on the roof anchor. Then clip the lanyard to the D-ring on the back of the harness. Squeeze the rope-grab and slide it along the safety rope to reposition the lanyard on the rope as you move around the roof.

6. **Relocate or remove** brackets by pounding up to slide them off the nails. Keep the lowest set of planks in place until you're done on the roof. Store tools and supplies in a bucket hung from a roof bracket.

Power tool safety

What's the best way to demonstrate really dangerous tool practices without taking the risk of hurting someone? With a crash test dummy, of course. It's just not easy to explain stupid techniques using words alone. That's where our dummy, Nigel, comes in!

Every year, emergency rooms report 120,000 visits for injuries caused by four tools: table saws, circular saws, nail guns and utility knives. Add to this the 200,000 ER visits for eye injuries—a large percentage of which occur during work around the house—and it's easy to see how we came up with this list of the most dangerous don'ts.

Our dummy, Nigel, is making some common mistakes that can result in severe injuries. But these are only a few examples of things not to do. Don't you be a dummy! When you start on your next project, keep these don'ts in mind so you don't become the next statistic.

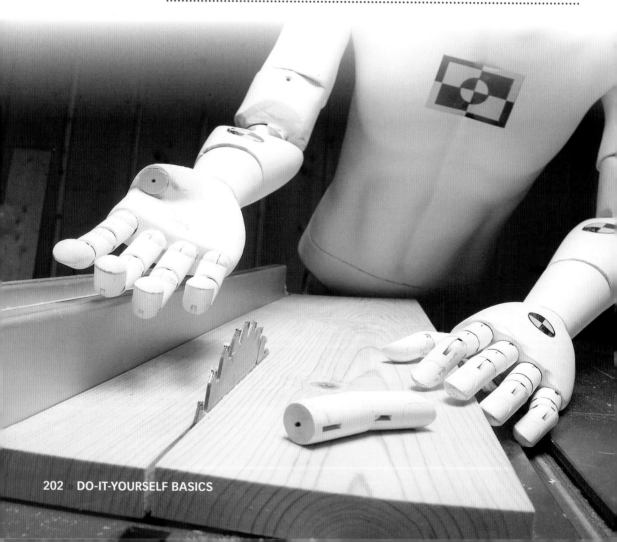

Don't crosscut against the table saw fence

Nigel the dummy is demonstrating one of the most dangerous table saw practices: cutting a board to length using the fence as a guide. There's a good chance the board will get pinched between the blade and the fence and get thrown back into his body with lots of force. That nasty incident is called "kickback." Broken thumbs, cracked ribs, ruptured spleens and punctured eyes are only a few of the resultant injuries you can suffer. About 35,000 people end up in the emergency room every year with table saw injuries, with 10 percent of them hospitalized. Industry experts estimate that about half of table saw injuries are caused either directly or indirectly by kickback.

In addition to avoiding the dangerous technique Nigel is using to crosscut a board, here are a few other ways to prevent kickback injuries:

> Don't cut anything that's longer than it is wide with the shorter side against the fence. If you want to crosscut with a table saw, use the miter gauge or a crosscutting sled. To learn how to build one, go to familyhandyman.com and search for "crosscutting sled."

> Avoid ripping wet, bowed or twisted lumber.

> Position your body to the right or left of the miter saw slots, not directly behind the blade.

> Don't let bystanders walk behind you when you're operating the saw.

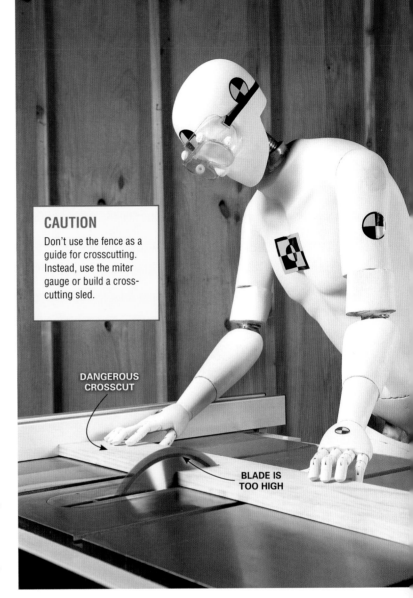

CAUTION
Don't use the fence as a guide for crosscutting. Instead, use the miter gauge or build a crosscutting sled.

DANGEROUS CROSSCUT

BLADE IS TOO HIGH

Don't remove that blade guard!

Every table saw sold includes a blade guard, which has a splitter attached. The guard covers the blade, preventing you from accidentally touching it, and the splitter keeps wood from pinching on the blade and kicking back. Don't take them off! Sure, the guard may be a nuisance at times, but it's better to be inconvenienced than to lose one or more fingers. Of the 35,000 emergency room visits we talked about earlier, 83 percent involve contact with the blade.

If you're buying a table saw, consider spending extra for the SawStop brand. It's the only saw on the market that stops the blade when skin touches it. If your blade guard is missing, contact the manufacturer for a replacement. An add-on guard like the HTC Brett-Guard is a good option if your original guard is missing or doesn't work well. If you don't want to spend the money, ask yourself what a finger is worth.

Even with a blade guard installed, you should keep your fingers away from the blade. Always use a push stick for rips less than 4 in. wide. If you're using your thumb to push the piece and the piece kicks back, you risk torn ligaments, tendons and broken bones. Push the cut piece past the blade, turn off the saw and wait for the blade to stop before retrieving the ripped piece. Don't reach near a spinning blade to remove a cutoff.

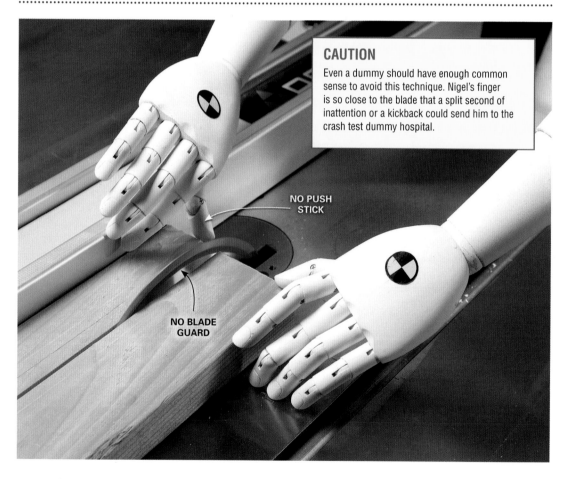

CAUTION

Even a dummy should have enough common sense to avoid this technique. Nigel's finger is so close to the blade that a split second of inattention or a kickback could send him to the crash test dummy hospital.

NO PUSH
STICK

NO BLADE
GUARD

Don't put your hand directly behind a circular saw

There are an estimated 14,000 visits to the emergency room every year as a result of circular saw injuries. Many of these injuries result in lost or severely damaged fingers. When you're using a circular saw, remember that if the blade binds, the saw can shoot backward a lot faster than you can move your hand out of the way. Anything in the blade's path, including fingers, hands, legs or feet, is in danger of getting cut. Avoid the risk by clamping your work and keeping both hands on the saw whenever possible. Also keep your body to the side of the saw rather than directly behind it.

CAUTION
Don't hold a board like this. Use a temporary nail or clamp instead. Nigel risks losing a finger or two if the saw binds.

DANGEROUS HAND POSITION

HAND TOO CLOSE

CAUTION

Don't hold a board close to the nail gun tip. Move your hand as far back as possible to avoid getting a nail through your finger.

Don't put your hands near a nail gun

Even if you're a nail gun expert, nails don't always go straight. Wood grain or knots can deflect the nail and cause it to shoot out the side of the board. If you're driving the nail at an angle to toenail a board, there's a good chance the nail can glance off and go shooting into space. If you must hold a board with your free hand, keep it well away from the nail gun muzzle. If you're reaching over a board to hold it down, move your hand out of the nail's path. Also avoid shooting into large knots that can deflect the nail. And, of course, always wear eye protection when you're using a nail gun.

Don't be sloppy with nail guns

You've all seen the news stories. X-rays of big nails embedded in someone's head, lodged in a spine or stuck in a foot. Ask any carpenter and you're sure to hear a story about a nail that went through a finger or hand. A tool that's powerful enough to shoot a 3-in.-long nail into wood can easily penetrate skin and bone. Depending on the type, some nail guns can be set to "bump-trip." In this mode, the operator can simply hold down the trigger and bump the nail gun nose against the surface to shoot a nail. This is great for speeding up jobs like nailing down plywood sheathing, but it creates a risk if you hold the trigger while carrying the nail gun. Bump your leg and you'll be heading to the emergency room. In incidents where accidental contact caused an injury, more than 80 percent of the time the operator had a finger on the trigger.

There are two ways to avoid this. First, get out your owner's manual and see if you can set your nail gun to sequential mode. This requires you to push down the muzzle and then pull the trigger for each nail. Second, keep your hand off the trigger when you're carrying a nail gun, or better yet, unplug the hose. Then there's no chance of accidental firing.

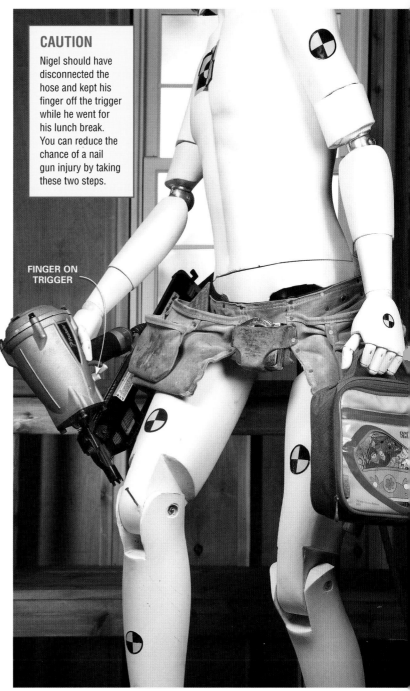

CAUTION

Nigel should have disconnected the hose and kept his finger off the trigger while he went for his lunch break. You can reduce the chance of a nail gun injury by taking these two steps.

FINGER ON TRIGGER

Don't get careless with a knife

Power tools are one thing, but did you know that utility knives are one of the most dangerous tools, accounting for a whopping 60,000 estimated emergency room visits a year? One slip is all it takes to put a deep cut in any body part that's in the way. And while most cuts are superficial and may only require a few stitches, permanent tendon and nerve damage is common.

The best way to avoid an injury is to clamp materials whenever possible to avoid having to hand-hold them. If you do have to hold something while you're cutting, imagine a line at right angles to the cutting line and keep your hand behind it (on the dull side of the blade).

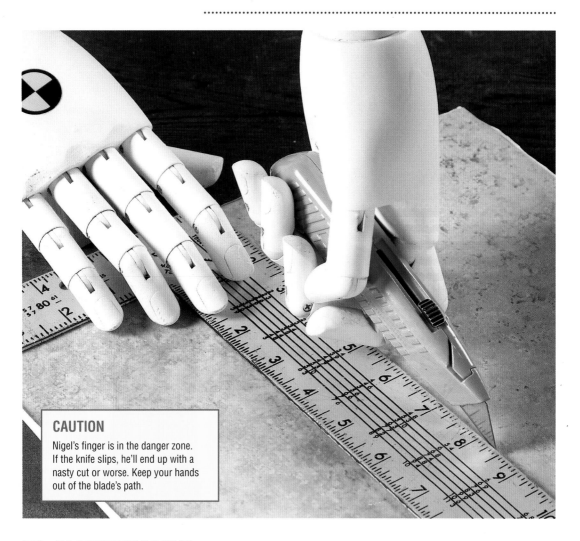

CAUTION

Nigel's finger is in the danger zone. If the knife slips, he'll end up with a nasty cut or worse. Keep your hands out of the blade's path.

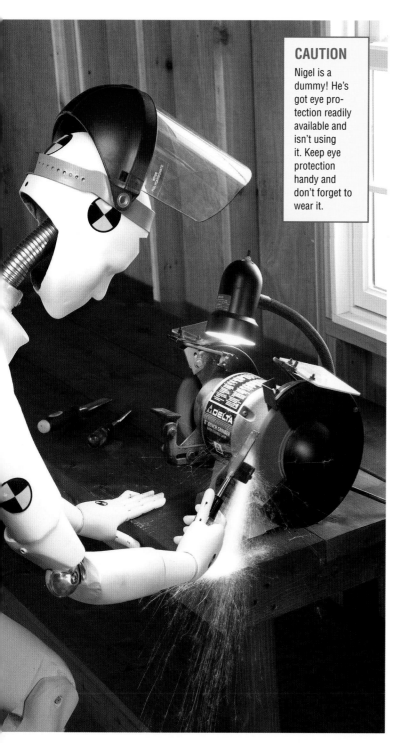

CAUTION

Nigel is a dummy! He's got eye protection readily available and isn't using it. Keep eye protection handy and don't forget to wear it.

Don't risk your eyes

It's hard to think of a good reason not to wear safety glasses, goggles or a face shield when you're working around the house. It's obvious that Nigel should be wearing his face shield. Of the more than 200,000 emergency room visits a year for eye injuries, at least 10,000 of them involve grinders. Browsing accident reports on the Internet will convince you of the risk. Wood chips, metal shards, bits of tile, household chemicals, paint, solvents and sticks are some of the things that injure eyes. The good news is that it's easy to protect your vision. Just choose the right eye protection for the task at hand. For general work around the house, wear ANSI-approved safety glasses or goggles. Look on the frame for the "Z87+" marking, which indicates that the glasses are rated for high impact. Wear a face shield for grinding operations. Buy several pairs of safety glasses and keep them in convenient locations so you'll always have them on hand.

Facts about radon

A decade ago, media hype caused both panic and skepticism about the risks and effects of radon. Now, better research has made two things clear: Elevated levels of radon over a long period of time can cause lung cancer, and there are effective ways to reduce these levels.

While questions still remain over the quantities and length of exposure, radon concerns are a fact of homeownership. Most residential real estate transactions require radon testing, and many states require radon mitigation for new construction. Here we'll help you figure out whether your home has risky radon levels and what you can do to reduce them.

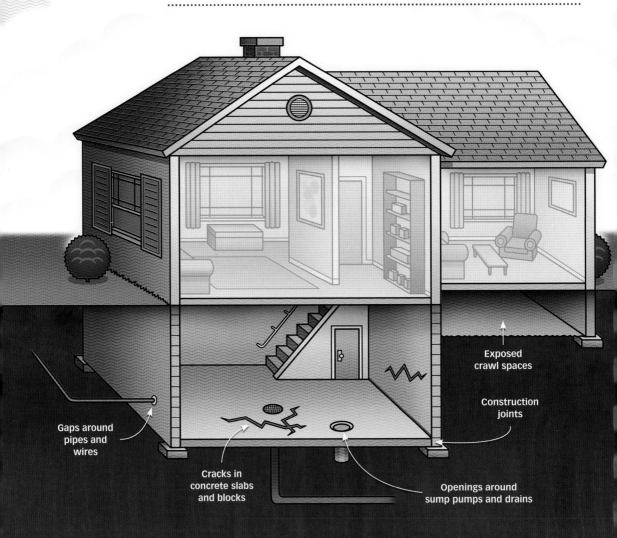

Gaps around pipes and wires

Cracks in concrete slabs and blocks

Exposed crawl spaces

Construction joints

Openings around sump pumps and drains

1. What is radon?

Radon is a colorless, odorless radioactive gas that's produced by decaying uranium. It's present in nearly all soils, and very low levels of radon are found in the air we breathe every day.

2. Why is it a problem?

The problem occurs when radon gas enters your home and gets trapped. Long-term exposure to high levels of radon can cause lung cancer.

3. How does it enter a home?

The gas moves from the soil into a home. Although it can seep directly through pores in concrete, the worst entry points are gaps in walls and floors. Any house, of any age, in any state can have elevated radon levels. It really depends on the way your specific house interacts with the surrounding soil. Your neighbor's radon level may differ significantly from yours.

4. How do I test for radon?

Conduct the test in the lowest livable area of your house that is regularly used eight to 10 hours per week.

Short-term tests are useful to see if further testing is warranted. Most are activated charcoal-based or electret ion that measure radon levels for two to seven days. You mail the tests to a lab for the results. Short-term tests are available at home centers, hardware stores and online retailers. Visit rtca.com for more information.

Long-term tests measure levels for 90 days to one year. Most, such as this AccuStar test, are based on alpha particle tracking. This is a more accurate indicator of average annual levels in your home, which can vary significantly from day to day and month to month based on factors such as a drop in air pressure, gusty winds, variable soil moisture, and snow cover, which traps radon gases.

The AccuStar test is available through state radon agencies, accustarlabs.com and online retailers.

Continuous electric monitors, such as the Safety Siren Pro Series digital meter, plug into a standard outlet. These monitors can be used for both short- and long-term testing and give you a running average. They use an ionization chamber and sample the air continuously. Consider sharing the monitor and costs with neighbors.

Safety Siren Pro Series 3 digital continuous radon meter

Radon Testing Corporation of America's short-term charcoal canister

AccuStar Alpha Track long-term radon test, $24

5. When should I take action?

The EPA recommends doing a second test if an initial short-term test registers 4 picoCuries per liter (pCi/L) or higher. A long-term test will give you the most accurate information, but a short-term test is acceptable if you need the results quickly, such as for a real estate transaction, or your first levels registered 8 pCi/L or higher.

If a second test registers above 4 pCi/L, consider taking steps to reduce radon levels in your home.

pro tips!

According to radon mitigation expert Val Riedman, a skilled DIYer can usually install a fan and exhaust system (see "The ultimate solution"). "I've helped hundreds of DIYers reduce their radon levels to acceptable levels," says Riedman. "And while installing a radon mitigation system isn't always a simple project, DIYers with the right information, a working knowledge of tools and an understanding of their home's construction techniques can install an effective system."

Riedman says houses that are good candidates for a DIY system have a basement that sits on top of a gravel base or have a sump system and drain tile. If you're not sure what's underneath your basement or you have a dirt crawl space, Riedman can walk you through testing and alternative mitigation scenarios. He offers free consulting advice and step-by-step guides to DIYers interested in buying radon fans and other specialized equipment from his site, indoor-air-health-advisor.com.

"If you're considering installing a radon mitigation system yourself," says Riedman, "it's very important to know what you're doing so you don't increase radon levels or cause combustion appliance backdrafting, which can increase carbon monoxide levels in your home."

Other good DIY resources are your state's radon office and the EPA's detailed guides at epa.gov/radon.

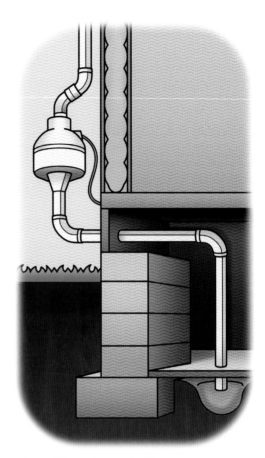

The ultimate solution

The most effective system is a vent pipe placed in the sump pit (if you have a sump pump) or a hole made under your concrete floor slab. A special in-line radon fan is placed in the attic or outside the house to draw air through the vent and radon from under the basement floor. The easiest method is to run the vent out the side of the house and up to the eaves as shown here. You can also run the vent up through the house and out the roof, which is a lot more work and cost, but it looks better.

Pros usually charge thousands of dollars to install a radon mitigation system, depending on your home and your radon levels. Your state radon office will have a list of qualified contractors.

6. How do I reduce radon levels?

Try these easy repairs to reduce radon levels. These efforts alone rarely reduce levels significantly, but if your level is only slightly elevated, these repairs might make the difference. They will also make other radon reduction methods more effective and cost efficient.

Once you've tackled these, retest. If levels are still high, consider installing a radon mitigation system yourself or hire a pro.

Don't panic

Act, but don't overreact. The risks from radon are cumulative, which means serious effects result from exposure to high levels over a long period of time. It is prudent to test radon levels and decide on a course of action. But you don't have to move out of your house or hire the first contractor who can fix the problem. For more information, contact your state radon office at epa.gov/radon.

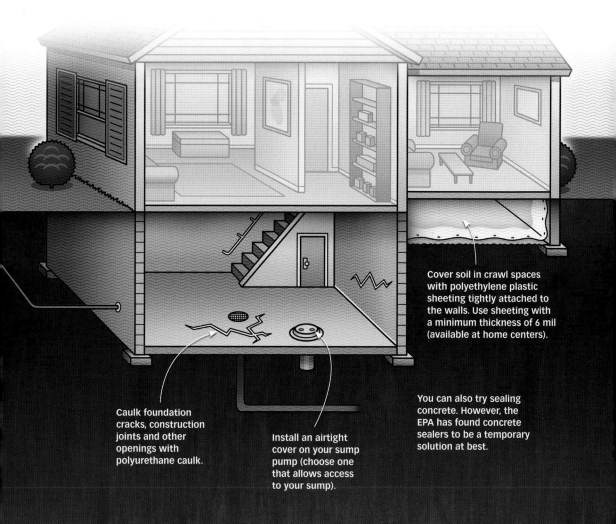

Cover soil in crawl spaces with polyethylene plastic sheeting tightly attached to the walls. Use sheeting with a minimum thickness of 6 mil (available at home centers).

Caulk foundation cracks, construction joints and other openings with polyurethane caulk.

Install an airtight cover on your sump pump (choose one that allows access to your sump).

You can also try sealing concrete. However, the EPA has found concrete sealers to be a temporary solution at best.

Chapter **8**
DIY Gifts You Can Make

Wooden phone stand

If you have a lot of people on your gift list, we've got you covered. Here's a simple item everyone will appreciate. And you can crank out 12 of them in an afternoon—finishing time included!

Choose any wood, any thickness

Our photos show how to make a device stand suitable for holding either a tablet or a phone. All you need is a length of wood of any species that's at least 3/4 in. thick. A 3-1/2-in.-wide board works fine for phones, but you'll need a minimum width of 5-1/2 in. to make a stand for a tablet. The cutting angles and steps are the same for any width or thickness.

We used walnut to make the phone stand shown here. But this would be the perfect project for an eye-catching exotic species like bubinga, teak or purple heart. They're all available at woodworking stores and online. With a project this small, you can get a beautiful, unique look without breaking the bank.

You'll need a table saw

This project involves cutting grooves **(Photo 1)**, ripping beveled edges **(Photo 3)** and cutting the stands to length **(Photo 4)**—tasks best done

1. Cut a test groove. Assemble a 3/8-in.-thick dado set in your table saw and adjust it to cut 3/8 in. deep and 1 in. away from the fence. Set the angle to 20 degrees, then cut a groove in a piece of 2x6 to test the fit of your devices.

TEST GROOVE

1

on a table saw. We cut beveled edges parallel on opposite sides, but you can cut opposing bevels or go with square edges and rout decorative profiles if you wish. The groove dimensions don't factor in any protective case you may have. They're just a starting point; you'll likely need to adjust them. The test shown in **Photo 2** will help you fine-tune the grooves.

Sand the boards first

If you're using construction or rough-sawn lumber, sand the top face of the boards up to 180 grit before doing any cutting. It's much easier than sanding small parts later. When you're done, spray on a finish of your choice. If you're in a hurry, shellac is a good choice because it dries quickly between coats.

2

Check the fit. Rest your devices in the groove. They should feel firmly secure when you tap the screens. If not, adjust the depth and/or width of the groove and retest until they do. When the fit is right, cut the groove in your project board.

20-DEGREE BEVELS

3

Rip the bevels. Set your saw's blade to 20 degrees. Cut parallel bevels on the edges of the board. A ripping blade is best for ripping solid lumber, but a combination blade is fine.

STOP BLOCK

MITER GAUGE

4

Cut to length. Crosscut the stands to length using a miter gauge with a stop block clamped to the saw's fence. Clamp it a few inches behind the blade. As you slide the workpiece past the block, there's a gap between the fence and the workpiece so it doesn't bind. Cut a bevel at the end of the board, then slide the beveled end against the block to cut successive stands to length.

5

Sand the edges. Glue sandpaper to a flat board using spray adhesive, and then sand all four beveled edges up to 180 grit.

Mosaic stepping-stones

Alice Medley loves to create works of art from the pebbles she collects. And she was generous enough to invite us into her garage workshop to show us how to make these beautiful pebble mosaic stepping-stones. She uses a "dry-set" technique that makes it easy to change or adjust the pattern as you go without having to dig the stones out of wet mortar.

In addition to showing you how to make these stepping-stones, we've included plans for an ingenious reusable wooden mold that Alice purchased from a North Woods carpenter. The initial investment for this project—about $60—gets you the plywood, a bag of mortar, pigment and muriatic acid. It's enough material to make about seven or eight stepping-stones. After that, each one will cost you less than a dollar.

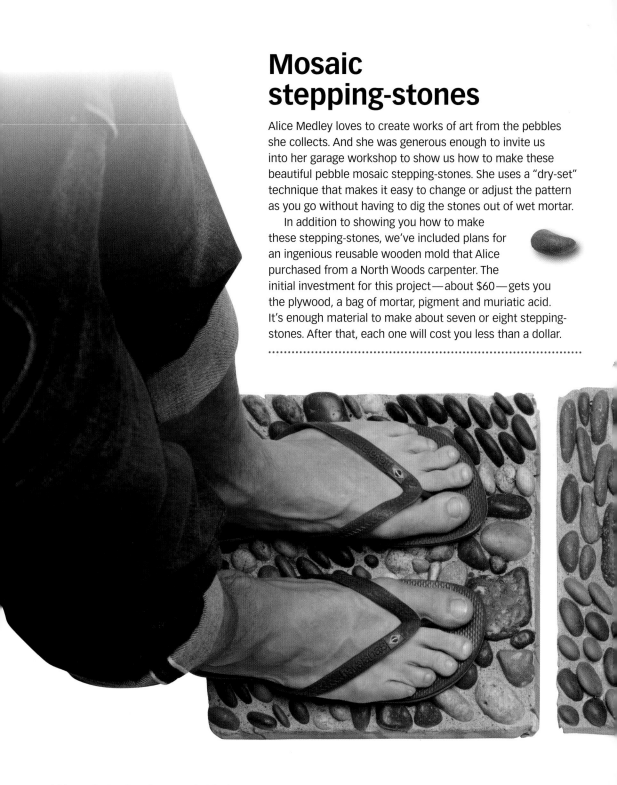

Build the mold

A small sheet of 3/4-in. plywood and some 1-1/4-in. screws are all you'll need to build the mold. Cut out the pieces according to the Cutting List. **Figure A** shows how the parts go together. When you're done, brush linseed or vegetable oil on the mold to protect it from moisture.

Start by collecting the stones

Alice collects her stones on the north shore of Lake Superior. You'll find similar stones in most parts of the country. Look for them in river and creek beds or along lakeshores. Wherever you find them, make sure you have permission and that it's legal to collect them. Another possible source is your local landscape supplier or wherever landscaping stone is sold.

Alice likes to sort them by color. She's got buckets and cans full of red, gray, white, brown and speckled stones. Keeping them sorted makes it a lot easier for her to find the right one as she creates a pattern.

Meet the Expert

Alice Medley started out using more traditional mosaic materials like tile and glass for her outdoor art projects. Then she discovered she could marry her love of stones with her love of mosaics. Alice learned this dry-mortar technique from Laura Stone, a stone mosaic artist from Minnesota. Alice has also created a 4-ft.-diameter, built-in-place pad for her backyard fire kettle using the same technique and is waiting to see how it holds up through harsh Minnesota winters.

Figure A
Stepping-stone mold
(forms 12" square steppers)

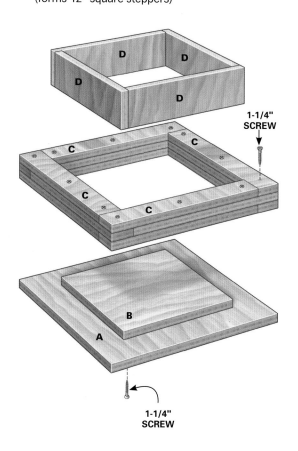

**1-1/4"
SCREW**

**1-1/4"
SCREW**

1

Assemble the mold. This plywood mold goes together quickly and comes apart easily after the mortar hardens. And you can use it again and again.

Assemble the stepping-stone

Photos 1–4 show the assembly steps. Alice likes to add a little brown pigment to the dry Type S mortar mix to give the stepping-stones a mellower look. You'll find cement pigments and Type S mortar at home centers and masonry suppliers. Or you can cheat like Alice does and just mix in a little colored ceramic tile grout. Make sure to wear rubber gloves to protect your skin from the mortar, which can cause skin burns.

You don't have to plan your pattern ahead of time. Alice says she has a design in mind and just starts arranging the stones. It's easier to start along the edges or in a corner and work toward the center, though. You'll have less fitting to do as you fill in the last few stones. Keep the stones close together and oriented with the long axis up and down. While it's tempting, Alice cautions against laying a stone flat. She says it doesn't look as good as you think it will and is more likely to pop out later. When you're done tamping the stones into the dry mortar, inspect the space between the stones to see if there are spots that require more mortar. They should be buried at least halfway. Fill sparse

2. **Spread dry mortar in the form.** Fill the plastic-lined form to about 3/4 in. from the top edge with dry Type S mortar. Level it with your gloved hand. It doesn't have to be perfectly flat.

3. **Arrange stones in a pattern.** The only rule is to keep the stones close together so they touch and stand up and are not laid flat.

4

Tamp the stones to level the tops. Lay a board across the stones and pound on it with a rubber mallet to embed the stones in the dry mortar and set the tops level with each other.

5

Sprinkle the stone. Adjust your spray wand or sprayer to the finest spray setting and sprinkle water over the completed stepping-stone to wet the mortar.

Materials List

Collection of small stones

One bag of Type S mortar mix

2' x 2' square piece of 6-mil poly

48" x 48" x ¾" plywood

Forty 1-1/4" corrosion-resistant screws

Optional items: mortar pigment or colored grout, muriatic acid and stone sealer

Cutting List

KEY	QTY.	SIZE & DESCRIPTION
A	1	18" x 18" x 3/4" subbase
B	1	12" x 12" x 3/4" base
C	12	2-1/4" x 15-3/4" x 3/4" frame
D	4	3-1/4" x 12-3/4" x 3/4" sides

areas with more mortar. Dust any dry mortar off the stones with a small brush.

The trickiest part of the process is wetting the mortar (**Photo 5**). We can't tell you exactly how much water to add, but it's better to sprinkle on several small doses than to get impatient and risk adding too much. Alice says the key is to alternate between wetting the top and tapping on the mold with the rubber mallet until it seems like not all of the water

6

Tap on the form. Tap on the form with the mallet to remove air and help the water penetrate. Continue sprinkling and tapping until it seems like no more water will be absorbed by the mortar.

7

Pull off the mold. Allow the stepping-stone to harden and cure for at least two days. Then carefully flip it over and remove the mold. Clean it with water and then acid if needed.

is being absorbed and bubbles quit appearing **(Photo 6)**. Expect to spend about 45 minutes sprinkling and tapping.

When the mortar is thoroughly dampened, set the completed stepping-stone in a shady spot and cover it with a damp cloth and plastic. Wait at least 48 hours before removing the mold.

After you remove the mold from the stepping-stone **(Photo 7)**, brush the stone off to remove any loose mortar and rinse it with clear water. If, after drying, the embedded stones have a film of mortar on them, clean it off with muriatic acid diluted according to the instructions on the container. Remember, always add acid to water, not the other way around, and wear rubber gloves and safety glasses.

To enhance the color of the stones, coat them with stone sealer. Alice recommends Sparks Stone Glamor sealer. You can find it online at sparkssw.com. Other brands will also work. You'll find stone sealers at home centers; masonry, landscape and tile suppliers; and online.

Stone-top table

The inspiration for this small end table came while browsing through a local tile store, looking at the huge variety of slate, granite, limestone and marble that's available. The table top shown here is 16-in.-square copper slate—a perfect match for the oak base—but many other stone tiles are available.

To make this table, you'll need a power miter saw, drill and hand tools. The stone top doesn't need cutting—just soften the sharp edges with 120-grit sandpaper. The base is made from standard dimension oak, available at home centers. And once you put together the simple cutting and assembly jigs shown in the photos on the next page, the table base almost builds itself.

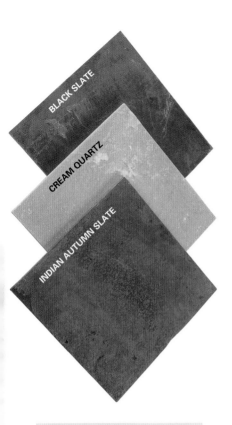

Figure A
Stone-top table

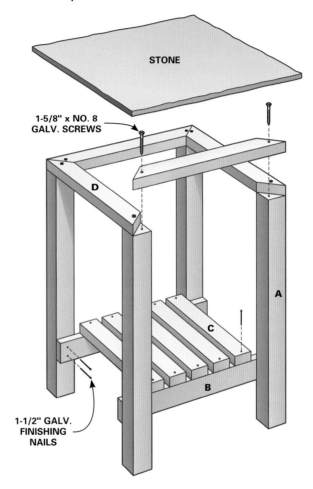

STONE

1-5/8" x NO. 8
GALV. SCREWS

D

A

C

B

1-1/2" GALV.
FINISHING
NAILS

Materials List

WOOD
| 2 | 2x2 x 3' oak |
| 14' | 1x2 oak |

Note: If the table is for outdoor use, use white oak or ash, which are more rot-resistant.

STONE TILE
| 1 | 16" x 16" x 1/2" |

HARDWARE
1 lb.	1-1/2" galvanized finishing nails
8	1-5/8" x No. 8 galvanized screws
4	Nylon chair glides
	Exterior wood glue
	Exterior construction adhesive

Cutting List

KEY	NAME	QTY.	DIMENSIONS
A	Leg	4	2x2 x 16-3/4"
B	Shelf supports	2	1x2 x 13-3/4"
C	Shelf slats	5	1x2 x 10-3/4"
D	Mitered top support	4	1x2 x 13-3/4"

1. Make a jig with square and mitered stop blocks screwed to a straight 1x4. Slide the 1x4 to the right length for each piece and clamp it down. When you cut the miters, set the saw for 45-1/2 degrees. That way, the outside corners of the top—the only part that shows—will be tight even if the top isn't perfectly square. Sand all the oak pieces before beginning assembly.

2. Set up a square assembly jig with 1x4s attached to your workbench. Use two shelf supports as spacers to ensure that the jig is the correct width. Set two table legs (A) in the jig and attach a shelf support (B) with glue and nails. Predrill with a 5/64-in. drill bit, or use one of the nails with the head clipped off as the drill bit.

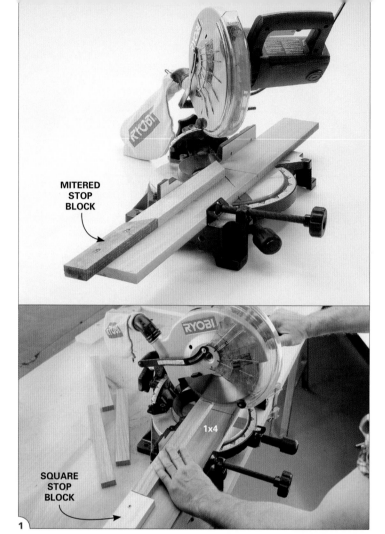

MITERED STOP BLOCK

1x4

SQUARE STOP BLOCK

1

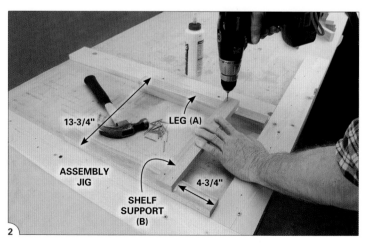

13-3/4"

LEG (A)

ASSEMBLY JIG

4-3/4"

SHELF SUPPORT (B)

2

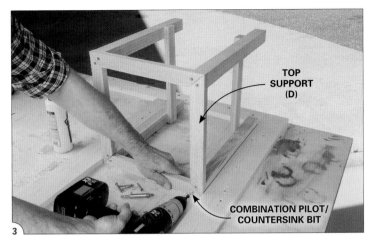

TOP SUPPORT (D)

COMBINATION PILOT/ COUNTERSINK BIT

3

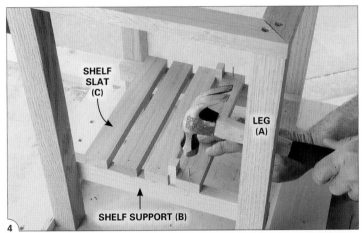

SHELF SLAT (C)

LEG (A)

SHELF SUPPORT (B)

4

CONSTRUCTION ADHESIVE

5

3. Screw down the mitered top supports (D) with the table still in the jig, using glue and 1-5/8-in. galvanized screws. Predrill and countersink with a combination bit at a slight angle, toward the center of the leg.

4. Predrill and nail the shelf slats with the legs tight and square against the sides of the assembly jig. Attach the center slat first, centering it on the shelf support. Wipe off excess glue and set the remaining slats, using two 1/2-in. spacers. Set the nails, fill the holes, then sand.

5. Glue the stone top to the base. First, center the table and trace the top onto the tile. Lay a bead of construction adhesive within the outline, keeping the glue away from the outer edge to avoid oozing. Press the table into the glue. Place a weight on the table for 24 hours until the glue sets. Leave excess glue until it's dry, and then peel it away. Finish the wood with exterior oil or varnish and add a nylon chair glide on the bottom of each leg.

Super-simple bench

One of the easiest ways to make a good garden even better is to set a comfortable bench in a secluded corner. Just having a place to sit transforms an ordinary patch of flowers into a quiet contemplative refuge.

So if you're looking for a simple bench, take a look at this one, based on a design by Aldo Leopold, whom many consider the father of wildlife ecology. Leopold's writings have led many to discover what it means to live in harmony with the land. If this bench was good enough for him, it's definitely good enough for the rest of us!

A little research led to this sturdy design which can be built quickly with a few 2x8s, glue and screws. Best of all, it's amazingly comfortable, perfect for bird-watching—even for two people.

22-1/2 DEGREE READING

LEG ASSEMBLY

17-1/4"

1

Mark one end of the 2x8 x 10 at a 22-1/2-degree angle with a speed square or protractor, then cut with a circular saw. Make a mark 36 in. away and repeat the cut at the same angle. Cut the remaining front leg and two back legs from the same piece. Cut the seat and the backrest from the 2x8 x 8.

2

Fasten the legs together. Stack and clamp the seat and backrest to the edge of the worktable as guides, and then align the legs against them. Spread adhesive on the front leg, set the rear leg in place, and fasten the legs together with three 2-1/2-in. screws.

Building tips

To make a simple project even simpler, remember these tips:

➤ Be sure to assemble the legs **(Photo 2)** so they're mirror images of each other, and not facing the same direction.

➤ Use clamps or a helper to hold the legs upright when securing the seat.

➤ Predrill all your screw holes to prevent splitting the wood.

Tools

Speed square or protractor
Drill with #8 countersink drill bit
Circular saw
Caulking gun

Materials list

1 2x8 x 8' cedar, redwood or treated lumber (seat and backrest)
1 2x8 x 10' cedar, redwood or treated lumber (front and rear legs)
Exterior construction adhesive
2-1/2" galvanized deck screws

17-1/4"

2-1/2" SCREWS

45"

42"

36"

3

Attach the seat and backrest. Stand the two ends up, 42 in. apart, spread glue on the tops of the rear legs, and screw the seat in place. Lay the bench on the worktable and attach the backrest with glue and screws.

Stair-step plant display

We tend to buy plants first and worry about good spots for them later. So unfortunately, many of the prettiest plants get lost in the corners of a deck and sunroom and don't get the attention (or the light) they deserve.

To help solve this problem and to spotlight some favorite plants, we came up with this simple display stand. It's made from cedar 1x2s that are cut into just two lengths, stacked into squares and nailed together. We used western red cedar with the rough-sawn side exposed. Assembly is simple and fast, because there's nothing to measure as you build—just keep everything square and use the wood pieces themselves for spacing and alignment.

Here's what you'll need

For supplies, you'll need seven 8-ft.-long cedar 1x2s, exterior glue, a few dozen 4d galvanized finish nails and some 100- or 120-grit sandpaper. You'll also need a hammer, a tape measure and a framing square, plus a saw that can cut the 1x2s to a consistent length. A power miter saw is great for this (you can rent one) but you could also use a handsaw in a miter box. An exterior finish for the wood is attractive, but not really necessary.

Begin by trimming any rough or out-of-square ends from your 1x2s. Almost all the ends will show, so they need to look good. Cut the 1x2s into sixteen 20-in. pieces and twenty-seven 10-3/4-in. pieces. It's important that the two groups of pieces are consistent in length, so rather than measuring each one, clamp a "stop block" to your bench the appropriate distance from the blade of your saw and push the 1x2 up against it for each cut.

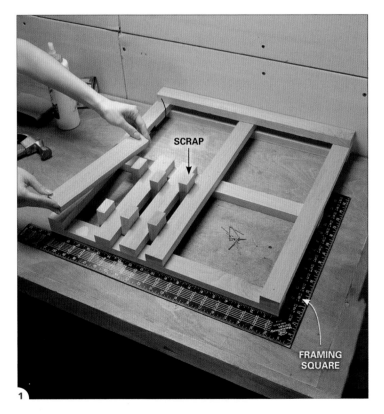

SCRAP

FRAMING SQUARE

1

1. Assemble the first two layers without nails or glue to get the spacing right and to make sure everything is square. Use scrap pieces of 1x2 as spacers. Once everything is square, glue and nail all the intersections.

How to build it

Begin making your stand by arranging the lowest two layers without nails or glue **(Photo 1)**. Lay out the bottom three 20-in. pieces against a framing square, then lay three more 20-in. pieces and three 10-3/4-in. pieces on top of them as shown in Photo 1.

Adjust the spacing, using scrap pieces to create the gaps, and make sure everything is square. The second layer should have a plant platform in one corner and nothing in the other three. When everything looks good, nail the pieces together, using one nail and a dab of glue at every intersection. Keep the nails 3/4 in. away from the ends of the boards to prevent splitting.

Add five more layers each consisting of two long and one short piece, with glue and a nail at every overlap. Check the sides with the square as you go to keep them straight. At the seventh layer, add two more platforms, with the 10-3/4-in. pieces running perpendicular to the pieces on the first platform. Add another five layers, with just two 10-3/4-in. pieces per layer, then fill in the top layer to create the final display platform **(Photo 2)**. When you're done nailing, sand all the outside edges of your stand and apply an exterior stain or preservative. Wait a few days for the finish to dry completely, then start moving in the plants!

2. Build up the stand "log-cabin style" until you get to the seventh layer, which has two platforms. When that's nailed down, continue until the 12th layer, which has the final platform.

SEVENTH LAYER

2

Figure A
Exploded view

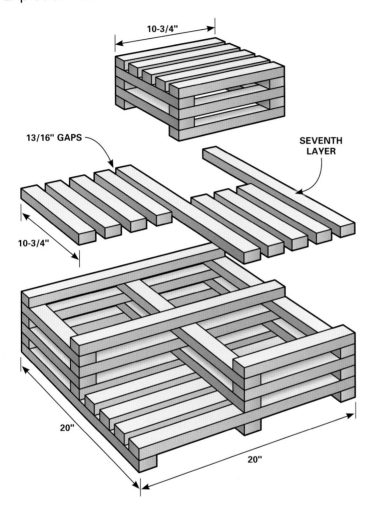

10-3/4"

13/16" GAPS

10-3/4"

SEVENTH LAYER

20"

20"

pro tips!

➤ Always nail at least 3/4 in. in from the end, and if the wood still splits, predrill the nail holes using a bit the size of the nail or the nail itself with the head snipped off. Your boards may also differ in thickness from those shown, which were 13/16 in. thick. If so, simply adjust the spacing between the boards.

Bonus Section

Transform It

Accent wall

This might be the easiest way to totally transform the look of a room. Once you've created your design using this simple glue-and-stick application, you can finish it up in a weekend.

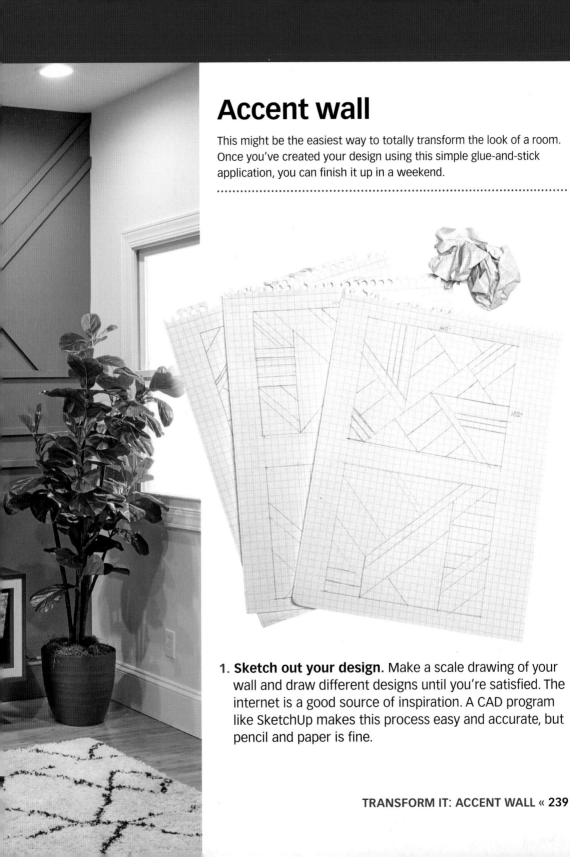

1. **Sketch out your design.** Make a scale drawing of your wall and draw different designs until you're satisfied. The internet is a good source of inspiration. A CAD program like SketchUp makes this process easy and accurate, but pencil and paper is fine.

2. **Paint the wall.** Choose your paint color and paint the entire wall. It's easier to paint it before the strips are attached, and the results look better too.

3. **Rip the strips.** Using your design plan, estimate how many linear feet of strips you'll need, and rip them to 1-1/4 in. wide on the table saw. We used 1/2-in. MDF because when ripped into thin strips, it's thick enough to create a shadow yet flexible enough to follow minor wall irregularities.

4. **Sand the strips.** A sharp corner doesn't hold paint well, so sand the sharp corners on the faces of each strip with a sanding block. It doesn't take much—just enough to turn the sharp corner into a tiny bevel.

5. **Paint the strips.** Spread out the strips on your work table and roll on a coat of primer. This is an important step with MDF; paint causes it to get really rough. Shellac-based primer is a good choice because it dries fast and sands very smooth. When the primer has dried, sand the strips with a 220-grit sanding sponge. Wipe off the dust and paint the strips. They'll probably require two coats.

6. **Locate the studs.** Find the studs and mark them with tape. We relied mainly on adhesive to hold the strips in place, but it's helpful to know where the studs are. If a strip needs a little more convincing to stay put, you can shoot a brad nail into a stud.

7. **Lay out the first strip.** Set up a laser level to get the long lines accurate. We used a self-leveling cross-line model from Skil. It doesn't shoot a 45-degree line, but if you use a large Speed square and the level's locking mechanism, you can set it at 45.

6

7

8. **Glue the first strip.** Cut the 45-degree angle on one end of the first strip, and then glue the back. Apply glue sparingly so the glue doesn't keep the strip from seating fully on the wall. We used a fast-grabbing construction adhesive (Loctite Power Grab) for this project. It has a fast initial tack, so it stays put as soon as you press it into place. If necessary, you can still shift it until it cures.

9. **Press the first strip into place.** Line up the strip with the laser line, and then press it against the wall. Since this first one is so long, tacking it on with a brad nail every 2 ft. will help keep it straight.

pro tips!

Living room–friendly miter saw

Running a miter saw in the house is a bad idea—it blows dust all over. But running to the shop for each cut doesn't make sense either. So, we made this simple "miter box" for a pull saw. First, make accurate 45- and 90-degree cuts on a 2x4 using a miter saw. Then, glue and nail these pieces to a scrap of plywood, using the saw's blade as a spacer. Now just clamp the miter box to a sawhorse right in the room where your accent wall is and make your cuts. No airborne dust, and no running back and forth to the shop!

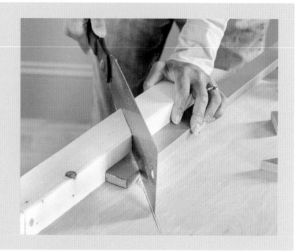

10. **Add the second strip.** The first line in our design requires two pieces, butt jointed together. Make the 45-degree cut on the second piece, hold it in place and then mark the butt joint. Cut the strip to length and glue it to the wall.

11. **Outline the big shapes.** Continue marking, cutting and attaching strips to outline the large shapes, as you did for the first piece. Use the laser level and adhesive, nailing where needed.

12. **Fill in the shapes.** Add the rest of the strips, proceeding from longest to shortest, filling in the large shapes.

13. **Finish up.** Fill any gaps or nail holes with spackling compound. When the spackling compound has dried, sand it smooth and touch up with paint.

12

13

pro tips!

If you need to tack a strip where there's no stud, shoot two brad nails at opposing angles—so they cross each other in the drywall—to hold the strip flat while the adhesive dries.

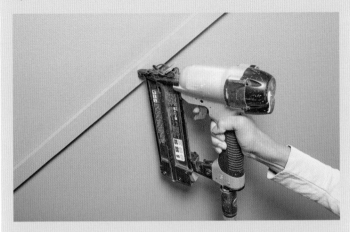

Materials List

1/2" x 48" x 96" sheet of MDF

1 gallon of paint

Spackling compound

Fast-tack construction adhesive

Brad nails

Deck over a worn-out patio

This was the ultimate bad patio: severely cracked and cratered, some areas raised by frost, others sunken after 50 years of settling. Originally, it was tiled, then the tile was chiseled off and the pockmarked surface got a coat of paint.

A slab with this much damage can't be fixed. But it can be covered up—and here we'll show you how. The results look just like a deck, but getting them is much easier and less expensive than building a deck from scratch. In most cases, this project is also less expensive than a new patio installed by a contractor. You could probably replace your worn-out patio yourself for less than the cost of this project, but DIY demolition and concrete pours are big, backbreaking jobs.

Before

Time, money and tools

Covering a patio with decking typically takes a weekend or two. This patio took much more time—five long days. That's partly because it's a big one (14 x 28 ft.). The grid pattern formed with different-colored decking also added a few hours to the job. But the biggest time factor was the unevenness of the patio surface. All those ridges and sunken spots meant hours of tedious shimming under the sleepers to form a flat surface for the decking **(see Photo 3)**.

The cost of this project depends mostly on the decking you choose. For looks and durability, we chose AZEK XLM decking, which is made from PVC. We used Harvest Bronze, with Walnut Grove as the accent color.

Aside from standard carpentry tools, you'll need a hammer drill for this project. You can get a hammer drill for less than $60 that will do the job. But consider spending $100 or more. Even a very small patio will require more than 50 holes, and a more powerful drill will make that chore

Will it work on your patio?

Even if your patio is in terrible shape, you can deck over it. Cracks, craters and seasonal movement along cracks are no problem. But beware of these three situations:

➤ If an area is badly cracked and sinks noticeably year after year, any decking you put over it will also sink and develop a low spot. In most cases, settling concrete stops sinking eventually, so delay this project until it does.

➤ This project raises the level of your patio by 2-1/2 to 3-1/2 in. (depending on the thickness of your decking and whether or not you put spacers under the sleepers). So any door thresholds adjoining the patio must be at least that far above the concrete. If not, this project won't work for you. If you live in a climate where the ground freezes, allow an extra 1/2 in. so that seasonal "frost heave" can raise the slab without damaging the threshold.

➤ Stairs connected to the patio can complicate this project. To keep step heights equal, you'll have to raise the treads by the same distance you raise the patio (2-1/2 to 3-1/2 in.). On concrete steps, that's a straightforward job: You can treat them just like the patio, screwing sleepers to the treads and risers and decking over them.

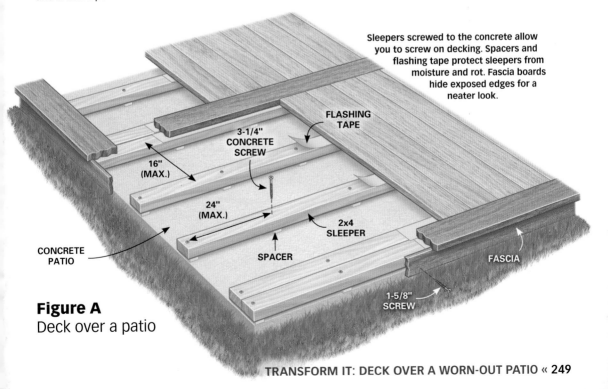

Sleepers screwed to the concrete allow you to screw on decking. Spacers and flashing tape protect sleepers from moisture and rot. Fascia boards hide exposed edges for a neater look.

FLASHING TAPE

3-1/4" CONCRETE SCREW

16" (MAX.)

24" (MAX.)

2x4 SLEEPER

CONCRETE PATIO

SPACER

FASCIA

1-5/8" SCREW

Figure A
Deck over a patio

SELF-LEVELING COMPOUND

Why use spacers?

You could lay your sleepers directly on the concrete, but we bought a 1/2-in.-thick PVC trim board and cut spacer blocks from it. Here's why:

➤ Spacers let you run sleepers parallel to the house so decking can run perpendicular to the house (if that's what you prefer). A patio typically slopes away from the house so that water runs off. If you run sleepers parallel to the house and set them directly on the concrete, each sleeper will block runoff. But with spacers, water can run under the sleepers.

➤ Spacers allow for longer decking screws. We wanted to use Cortex screws, which come with cover plugs made from the same material as the decking. They're easy to use and almost invisible. But they're 2-3/4 in. long; that's too long to sink into our decking if we use sleepers only.

➤ Spacers let the sleepers dry out. If kept damp, common grades of treated wood will eventually rot. Spacers keep the sleepers off the damp concrete so they can dry.

Solve water problems first

This corner of the patio had settled by more than 2 in. over the years. That meant a big reservoir after rain—and water in the basement. So we filled the reservoir with exterior-grade self-leveling compound. After the first batch hardened, we poured on a thin coat and gave it a slight slope so water would run away from the house.

Self-leveling compound hardens fast, so you can get on with the project. But it's also expensive. If you're not in a rush, you can get similar results for less than one-third the cost with concrete topping mix such as Sakrete Top 'n Bond or Quikrete Sand/Topping Mix.

We also took a couple of other water-fighting steps. To prevent water from seeping down along the foundation, we caulked the gap between the patio and the house. At the other end of the patio, a corner of the slab had sunk slightly below the level of the soil and rainwater pooled there. To correct that, we shaved off the sod with a spade, dug out a couple of inches of soil and replaced the sod.

a lot easier. Also consider buying an impact driver. Impact drivers pack a lot more torque than standard drills or drivers and will drive concrete screws much better. Most models are cordless, but you can get a corded model for less than $70 online.

Plan the layout

The layout of your sleepers will depend on the layout of your decking. If you want a standard decking design—all the deck boards running one direction—all you need are rows of parallel sleepers. If you want a more complicated decking pattern, like the one shown here, you'll need doubled sleepers to support any boards that run perpendicular to the others **(Figure A)**. We also installed sleepers to support the steps we later added to the concrete stoop **(Photo 1)**.

Lay the sleepers

The sleepers don't have to be level—they can follow the slope of your patio. But they do need to form a flat plane. If your patio is in good shape, you'll get a flat plane automatically. If your patio

SLEEPER
LOCATION

STEPS

1

SPACER

2

1. **Start with a layout.**
   Mark the sleeper loca-
   tions on the patio. Don't
   forget about extra sleepers to support stairs or
   railings.

2. **Predrill for concrete
   screws.** Drill through
   sleepers, spacers and
   into the concrete with a
   hammer drill, then drive
   in concrete screws. Overhang the sleepers along
   one edge of the patio and
   trim them to exact length
   later.

has ridges and sunken areas, you'll spend lots of time fussing with shims.

To preview the situation, lay a straight board across the patio in a few spots. Look for the highest hump in the patio and fasten your first sleeper there. Then work outward from the high spot, adding sleepers and checking for flatness along each sleeper and across them. Add shims to raise low spots.

Screwing down sleepers with concrete screws **(Photo 2)** is simple, but there are some things to keep in mind:

> Screws should penetrate the concrete by at least 1 in., so 3-1/4-in. screws are perfect. In low spots, where we had to stack up shims, we switched to 3-3/4-in. screws.

> As you drill, dust compresses around the drill bit. That slows you down, strains your drill and overheats the bit. To clear the dust, pull the bit completely out of the hole once or twice while drilling each hole.

> Drill the holes 1/4 to 1/2 in. deeper than the screw will reach. Extra depth provides a space for dust and grit, so screws are easier to drive.

> Have extra drill bits on hand. As a bit wears, it doesn't just drill more slowly; it also bores a slightly smaller hole and screws become harder to drive. We replaced each bit after about 40 holes.

continued on p. 254

Keeping it simple

If you're a beginning DIYer, don't let all the details on our deck scare you away. Your project can be a whole lot easier if you choose a simple decking design like the one shown here. With all the deck boards running in the same direction, all you need are sleepers centered 16 in. apart. You won't need to do the careful measuring required by our design, or make angled miters and other fussy cuts. A simple deck design makes this project almost impossible to get wrong.

If you have a badly uneven patio like ours, flattening the sleepers with shims **(Photo 3)** may take hours. It's tedious but not complicated.

You can slash the cost by using treated wood deck boards instead of manufactured decking. And if you live in a drier climate where the sleepers won't stay damp, you can skip the spacers and flashing tape.

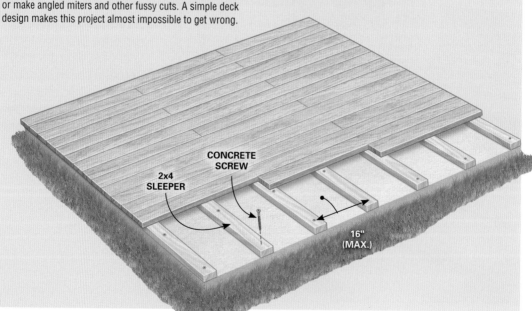

CONCRETE
SCREW

2x4
SLEEPER

16"
(MAX.)

Cover-ups for a cracked patio

Bury it under pavers

A concrete slab provides a firm, stable base for pavers. Cover the patio with a thin layer of sand, lay pavers over it, and the results look like a standard paver patio. It's a fairly simple project and the cost is reasonable, but expect a weekend or two of hard labor. For complete step-by-step instructions, go to familyhandyman.com and search for "cover patio."

Hide it under a rug

The quickest way to hide damaged concrete—or just add color—is with an outdoor area rug. They're available in a huge range of colors, designs and prices. The largest rugs are typically 9 x 12 ft. That may not cover your entire patio, but just covering most of an ugly patio makes a huge difference. Shop online or visit a store that handles patio accessories.

Snap-together tiles

Interlocking plastic tiles simply snap together; no need to fasten them to the patio. Some versions are plastic only. Others are topped with wood, ceramic or stone. (Ceramic or stone tiles require a flat surface—they may crack if installed over ridges or depressions.) To browse online, search for "deck tile" or "patio tile."

More ways to improve a patio

Whether your patio is in bad shape or just bland, there are many ways to revive it. But before you weigh your options, there's one thing to consider...

The crack factor

Cracks in your patio drastically limit your options. That's because cracks tend to move. Some grow wider over time, while others shrink and widen as the soil freezes and thaws. Some become uneven as one side of the crack sinks. Any movement happens so slowly that it's hard to detect. But if you know—or even think—that you have moving cracks, you have to choose a patio upgrade that can "float" over moving cracks without becoming damaged.

continued from p. 252

When all the sleepers are screwed down, take a few minutes to double-check for flatness. Set a 4-ft. straightedge on each sleeper, both across it and along it. If you find spots that are 1/16 in. or more out-of-plane, back out the screw and add or remove shims **(Photo 3)**.

Install the decking

Before decking, we covered the sleepers with flashing tape. Without it, water soaks the tops of the sleepers and the decking prevents the wood from drying. Common grades of treated lumber will rot if kept permanently damp, and flashing tape is the best insurance against that.

Installing deck boards over sleepers is just like installing them over standard deck framing **(Photo 4)**. We began with the

3. **Screw down and flatten the sleepers.**
   Check for flatness with a straightedge. Raise low spots with shims. At high spots, skip the spacer; stack up shims instead.

STRAIGHT-EDGE

PLASTIC SHIM

3

FLASHING
TAPE

4

darker "accent" boards, screwing them into place temporarily to act as guides for the "field" boards. When we reached the end of the deck, we removed the center divider board and cut it to final length. Then we removed and mitered the border boards and trimmed the sleepers to final length.

To cover the ends of the sleepers, we used a deck "fascia" board made from 1/2-in.-thick PVC. We cut the fascia into strips and screwed them to the sleepers.

4. Lay the decking. Install the deck boards just as you would on a standard deck. When you reach the end of the patio, position the last board, mark the overhanging sleepers and trim off the excess.

Materials List

Aside from the decking, here's an estimate of what you'll need to cover 100 sq. ft. of patio. Exact quantities depend on the shape of your patio and the layout of the decking.

➤ 90 linear ft. of treated 2x4
➤ 90 linear ft. of flashing tape
➤ Sixty 3/16" x 3-1/4" concrete screws
➤ 1/2"-thick PVC trim or deck fascia (for spacers), plastic shims, 3/16-in. masonry drill bits (minimum drilling depth of 3-1/2 in.)

Projects for a crack-free patio

Stain it

A coat of stain followed by a coat of sealer transforms a patio in a weekend. But there are downsides: You'll have to reseal every one to three years and may eventually have to restain it. Also, stain won't hide damage, and any repairs will likely show through the stain. To see how to apply stain in multicolor patterns, go to familyhandyman.com and search for "stain patio."

Tile it

A concrete patio is a great foundation for tile. And tile is a great way to turn a bland patio into a showpiece. The cost depends mostly on the tile you choose. Freezing water can destroy outdoor tile. So if you live in a climate that freezes, pay extra attention to the details. For the complete story, go to familyhandyman.com and search for "tile patio."

Resurface it

With a coat of resurfacer, you can make an old patio look like new concrete in a day. Just mix the cement-based powder with water and spread it over the patio. You can repair cracks and resurface over them, but the cracks may return. Quikrete Concrete Resurfacer and Sakrete Flo-Coat are two common brands.

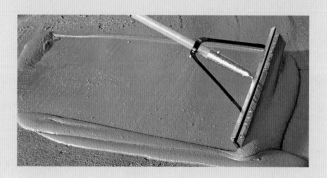